THE CHRISTMAS BOOK

EVE HARLOW

BCA

LONDON   NEW YORK   SYDNEY   TORONTO

Acknowledgements

The publishers thank the following who were
concerned in the preparation of the book.

Art Editor Alyson Kyles
Co-ordinating Editor Marilyn Inglis
Editor Diana Vowles
Production controller Shane Lask

Special photography by Duncan McNicol
(except page 5 Spike Powell)
Stylists Marie O'Hara, Allison Williams
Food prepared for photography by Nicola Palmer, Sarah Bush
Artwork illustrations Hayward & Martin
Recipe consultant Catherine Redington

We would also like to thank the following organisations
for their kind permission to reproduce the
photographs in this book:

Mary Evans Picture Library 6, 7 (Illustrator Fedor
Funzler from Glückliche Kinderzeit); Spectrum
Colour Library 4.

This edition published 1994
by BCA
by arrangement with Reed Illustrated Books Ltd
© Reed Illustrated Books 1986

CN 3935

Printed in Italy by
Rotolito Lombarda S.p.A Milan

· CONTENTS ·

NOTE

Standard spoon measurements are used in all recipes

1 tablespoon (tbls) = one 15 ml spoon
1 teaspoon (tsp) = one 5 ml spoon
All spoon measures are level

All eggs are sizes 3 or 4 (standard) unless otherwise stated.

For all recipes, quantities are given in both
metric and imperial measures. Follow either set
but not a mixture of both, as they are not interchangeable.

THE CHRISTMAS BOOK
·MAKING LIGHT OF CHRISTMAS·

Christmas and New Year can be the most wonderful family holiday, with the excitement and anticipation building up over the weeks before, the smell of rich food, fragrant greenery, the sparkle and glitter of tinsel – and the mysterious packages which are whipped away as soon as you enter a room. The secret of the kind of Christmas everyone remembers with pleasure is planning ahead.

The end of November is not too soon to begin Christmas, or start even earlier if possible. It is part of the fun, will save you worry, panic and exhaustion – and may even save you money.

The party plan

First, plan how you hope to spend Christmas. Do members of the family usually come to you? Have you a mixture of old and young people to cope with? Is a party for local friends part of this year's Christmas festivities, and will you feed them, or just give them nibbles? Are you likely to be invited out for at least one of the feast days?

Invitations, therefore, must be the first priority in planning for Christmas and New Year, so get them out – or reply to those extended to you – as soon as possible. Once the holiday 'diary' is filled in, you can begin to plan the biggest job – catering.

The Christmas holiday generally means a three-day Christmas, a weekend somewhere in between, and New Year at the end of the holiday. You can plan, if you're staying at home, on at least 10 festive meals over the holiday period, to say nothing of the odd snacks for friends who unexpectedly drop in.

Nobody wants to see the hostess constantly in the kitchen tired and flustered, with the spirit of Christmas quite obviously missing. The perfect holiday is one where the cook joins in the celebration.

Your supermarket will begin to stock and display special Christmas foods from November. Get into the habit of taking a notebook with you when you shop, and note the special lines, to see how items fit into your forward planning, and where certain foods can save time, preparation and effort.

Economical and efficient catering also depends on making maximum use of kitchen equipment. If your food processor, mixer or blender usually lives on a shelf or in a cupboard, bring it into a more convenient place, so that you can use it more often.

The menus in this book provide a variety of different kinds of foods, with something for every kind of taste – and budget. Each chapter also gives a work plan, showing you what can be done in advance. Even if you are not using all the menus in this book, the plans will be a guide to the kinds of dishes you should be planning to cook for the freezer, to save you time and effort later. Cakes and puddings, flans and sponges, soups, pâtés, sauces, stuffings, gravies, biscuits, scones, icecreams and sweets, and some standby meat and fish dishes are all suitable for forward freezer cooking.

The last Sunday before Advent is, in some parts of the country, still called Stir-up Sunday, when the cakes and Christmas puddings are mixed and cooked. To produce the best-tasting cakes and the most succulent puddings, plan to do your mixing on the Saturday before Stir-up-Sunday. With your menus outlined, and certain dishes marked for pre-cooking and freezing, you can take a look at the other areas of planning ahead for Christmas.

Choirboys singing carols are one of the most well-loved features of Christmas-time.

A table laden with the Christmas feast is truly a tempting sight.

Cards and posting

Christmas cards used to be sent only to those people we didn't see very often, or those we wished to particularly greet, or thank, for services during the year. These days, cards are sent to just about everybody – even the neighbours living next door, and the friends seen every day at the office. However, friends and family living far away must have priority in your forward plan because the last week in November is usually the date for mail going out of Europe, and the first week in December the date recommended for European posting. Updating the Christmas card list, buying the cards, (early buying provides the best designs), and posting them now, will be one more job you can tick off your list.

Gifts and gift wraps

Every year, we tell ourselves that next time we are going to buy Christmas gifts through the year and spread the cost and get better choice. This is pre-planning par excellence – but you probably didn't do it. If you can decide, choose, buy and wrap gifts for family and friends at least four to five weeks before Christmas, with the odd, unexpected purchases left to the last two weeks, you will have ticked off the second most time-consuming job of Christmas. In the Loving and Giving chapters, you will find some ideas for gifts from the kitchen. These are still the best kinds of gifts to receive, no matter what age the recipient, from the elderly to the very young, and these special gift foods can be fitted in with your own festive fare cooking.

Similarly, a hamper of delicious, unusual and mouth-watering food is a superb present for anyone – from a small basket of foreign cheeses to a large basket containing everything needed for 'instant' Christmas. From your shopping notes, list hamper contents that seem most suitable for the recipient, and buy items along with your normal shopping from November onwards.

Christmas papers and gift ties begin

Father Christmas first came into his own as a popular figure in Victorian times.

to appear several weeks before Christmas and are worth buying early, both for the wider choice of design available, and sometimes for economy. Christmas merchandise can often become more expensive the nearer to Christmas. Children should, if possible, try and make their own Christmas cards. Supply them with suitable cartridge paper, felt tipped pens or painting crayons, stick-on motifs, quick-stick glue and some glitter dust, the first day the Christmas school holidays begin. Similarly, they can be encouraged to make Christmas gifts – three to four weeks is not too much time for children to plan and execute something they'll be pleased with.

Begin to store suitable boxes for gift packing – check supermarket throw-outs, and look carefully at the boxes when you buy foods and household items. If they are strongly made, they can be covered with Christmas paper.

Tables and tableware

If you are planning parties, check the crockery, glasses, knives, forks and spoons well in advance, to see if anything needs to be borrowed or purchased. If a buffet party is part of your plans, have a dummy run and see if the bowls, serving dishes, plates etc. will fit onto the table you will be using. Glasses can be hired for parties, but the sooner you get your order in, the better.

Drinks and drinking

Spirits and wines are probably the most expensive item in the Christmas shopping list. It is well worth while looking for special end-of-bin offers in supermarkets and wine stores from the end of summer. These days, more and more people are being thoughtful about drinking and driving, so why not plan more punches, mulls and cups for your guests? These became very popular towards the end of the 18th century when Hogarth was recording the appalling drunkenness of the common people. The well-to-do decided that diluted drinks were more fashionable, and these drinks are having a similar popularity today, at the end of the 20th century, as people become more aware of the need for safety on the road.

Three weeks to go

This is a good time to start the decorations for the house, so look through the balls and baubles to see if new items are required and perhaps make a few new ones for the tree and table. Crackers should be purchased now, particularly if you are looking for really good contents. The best-looking, and the best value, go early.

Rooted Christmas trees, already potted, can sometimes be found in garden centres just before Christmas and they are worth buying, even though they are a little more expensive than the cut trees available later. Keep them well-watered, transplant to the garden after Christmas, and watch them grow for next year.

From now until Christmas week, you should begin to plan fresh food purchases such as green vegetables and fruit as some of them can be prepared for the freezer, saving preparation time later.

Two week run-up

Take the chance to do any advance work around the house that you can, to keep basic housework to a minimum over the Christmas holiday – it is the last thing you will want to be bothered with over such a busy period! If you are buying presents for pets, you should get them now – you will find that pet shops have very little left in the last few days to Christmas. Before things get too hectic, work out with the family how you will be using greenery around the house. If you wish to see special friends before Christmas, now is a good time.

One week to Christmas

This is a good time to confirm the arrival times of your guests, and which friends are likely to be coming for drinks and when. The greenery for the house should be purchased – or cut – this week, and an evening set aside for the traditional dressing of the Christmas tree.

If you are going to want fresh flowers, order them now ready to collect the day before Christmas Eve. Last minute supermarket shopping should be for perishables only because everything else is either in your freezer by now, or in your store cupboard. Happy Christmas!

The decorating of the tree is one of the most well-loved Christmas rituals.

THE CHRISTMAS BOOK
• FESTIVE FARE •

The Christmas holiday, from Christmas Eve to New Year's Day, adds up to 9 days of catering and can mean 27 meals. To encompass the range of dishes you will need, meal preparation needs to be pre-planned during the six weeks up to Christmas, if everything is to run smoothly without the cook being overworked and harassed.

Festive foods such as puddings, cakes, stuffing, biscuits and mincemeat can be made or prepared ahead, together with standby dishes, quiches, flans, mousses, pâtés and soups.

PORK AND PORT PÂTÉ
Serves 8

1 large onion
1 garlic clove
450 g (1 lb) belly pork
small glass of port
1 tsp fresh mint, chopped
salt and pepper
225 g (8 oz) lamb's liver, finely chopped
3 rashers streaky bacon, finely chopped
50 g (2 oz) mushrooms, finely chopped
1 egg, beaten
rosemary sprig, to garnish

Process or mince the onion, garlic and pork together. Mix in the port and mint, season to taste and leave to marinate in the refrigerator overnight.

Heat the oven to 180°C, 350°F, Gas Mark 4. Mix in the liver, bacon and mushrooms. Stir in the egg. Place in a foil-lined loaf tin and bake in the oven for 1½ hours. Pour off the fat and leave to cool. To freeze, fold the foil over the pâté and freeze in the tin for up to 2 months. To serve, remove the pâté from the tin in the foil, thaw at room temperature on absorbent kitchen paper in the foil. Garnish with a sprig of rosemary.

CROISSANTS
Makes 10

150 g (5 oz) butter
150 ml (¼ pint) warm milk
1 tsp salt
1½ tbls sugar
15 g (½ oz) dried yeast
2 tbls warm water
350 g (12 oz) strong white plain flour
1 egg yolk, beaten with a little milk

Put 25 g (1 oz) of the butter into a bowl and pour on the warm milk. Add the salt and sugar and mix. Leave to cool.

Blend the yeast with warm water. Leave to stand for 10 – 15 minutes until bubbling on top.

Add the yeast to the butter and milk, then gradually add the flour to make a soft dough.

Place the dough in a lightly greased polythene bag. Put aside in a warm place for 2 hours to rise.

Knead the dough until smooth and elastic, then put it into the refrigerator and chill for 1 hour.

Roll the dough out into a rectangle, and spread the remaining butter over the dough. Fold the dough twice and roll out again. Put back into the refrigerator and chill for 1 hour. Then roll, fold and roll again. Repeat this once more.

Heat the oven to 220°C, 425°F, Gas Mark 7. Roll the dough out to 1 cm (½ inch) thickness and cut into 5 squares. Cut each square into 2 triangles. Roll the triangles up, starting with the longest edge and roll towards the point. Bend the croissant into a crescent shape.

Put the croissants on to a floured baking sheet and brush with beaten egg and milk. Bake in the oven for 15 minutes. Leave to cool. To freeze, pack into rigid boxes. Store for up to 6 weeks. To serve, heat from frozen on a baking sheet for about 15 minutes at 180°C, 350°F, Gas Mark 4.

MINCE PIES
Makes 20

350 g (12 oz) shortcrust pastry

350 g (12 oz) mincemeat

50 g (2 oz) granulated sugar

Heat the oven to 200°C, 400°F, Gas Mark 6. Roll out two-thirds of the pastry and cut into 20 rounds 7.5 cm (3 inches) in diameter. Use them to line greased tartlet tins and fill them two-thirds full of mincemeat. Dampen the edges.

Roll out the remaining dough and cut out 20 rounds 6 cm (2½ inch) in diameter. Put them on top and press lightly together to seal. Sprinkle each pie with sugar.

Bake in the oven for 20 minutes or until golden brown.

Clockwise from top: Light and lovely Christmas cake; Christmas shortbreads and Mince pies; Pork and port pâté; Croissants; Spinach flan; Chicken liver flan; Centre: Yule log

Ready for the freezer, clockwise from top: Turkey and onion soup; Country-style turkey pie; Spinach flan; Mince pies; Chicken liver flan; Pork and port pâté

Freezing Poultry

Wash the bird inside and out and pat dry with kitchen towel. Wrap cling film or foil round the extremities, then enclose the whole bird in foil and finally a freezer bag, checking the legs and wings have not punctured it. Storage times are: turkey 10 – 12 months; chicken 10 – 12 months; duck 4 – 6 months; goose 4 – 6 months.

THAWING POULTRY

You must be careful to check that poultry is *completely* thawed before cooking. Thawing times are:

under 3.5 kg (8 lb)	24 – 36 hours
3.5 – 6.25 kg (8 – 14lb)	36 – 48 hours
6.25 – 9 kg (14 – 20 lb)	48 – 60 hours
over 9 kg (20 lb)	72 hours

Thaw in the wrapping in the refrigerator. The flesh should be soft to the touch and there should be no ice crystals left in the cavity.

CHICKEN LIVER FLAN

225 g (8 oz) shortcrust pastry
For the filling:
225 g (8 oz) chicken livers
50 g (2 oz) unsalted butter
1 tbls vegetable oil
salt and pepper
2 celery sticks
225 g (8 oz) mushrooms, sliced
3 tbls lemon juice
1 tsp cornflour
a little cold water
50 g (2 oz) mild cheddar cheese, grated

Heat the oven to 200°C, 400°F, Gas Mark 6. Roll out the pastry to line a flan ring and bake blind in the oven for 12–15 minutes.

For the filling, cut the chicken livers into small pieces and quickly sauté in a little butter and oil. Remove from the pan and season to taste.

Put more butter and oil into the pan and sauté the celery and mushrooms until the celery is soft. Add the lemon juice and then the cornflour mixed with a little water.

Put the chicken livers in the base of the flan case, then pour the mushroom mixture over the top. Sprinkle with grated cheese. Bake in the oven for 15–20 minutes. Leave to cool.

Open freeze, then wrap in foil or polythene, or pack into boxes. Store 1 – 2 months. To serve, unwrap and reheat from frozen in a moderate oven, 180°C, 350°F, Gas Mark 4 for 40 minutes.

Variations:

Mushroom Cook a chopped onion in a little butter until soft and golden. Stir in 225g (8 oz) chopped mushroom and a little lemon juice. Cool, and stir in 2 beaten eggs and 150 ml (¼ pint) half cream. Season and mix in 1 tsp of chopped fresh parsley. Pour the filling into the pre-baked case and bake in the oven at 180°C, 350°F, Gas Mark 4 for 40 minutes.

Spinach Put 750 g (1½ lb) washed, shredded spinach in a pan with a little butter. Cook for about 10 minutes, then drain and press out any water. Put into a bowl and mix in 2 beaten eggs and 225 g (8 oz) low fat soft cheese. Season to taste and sprinkle with grated nutmeg and 1 – 2 tbls Parmesan cheese. Pour the filling into the pre-baked case and bake in the oven at 180°C, 350°F, Gas Mark 4 for 40 minutes.

CHRISTMAS SHORTBREADS

Makes 12 biscuits

100 g (4 oz) unsalted butter
50 g (2 oz) caster sugar
150 g (5 oz) plain flour
25 g (1 oz) rice flour
caster sugar, to decorate

Heat the oven to 180°C, 350°F, Gas Mark 4. Place the butter and sugar in a bowl and cream together until fluffy. Sift in the flours and work to form a soft dough. Knead lightly until smooth.

Roll the dough into a log shape, wrap in polythene and chill for 30 minutes. Cut the roll in slices and place on a greased baking sheet. Bake in the oven for 15 – 20 minutes until golden round the edges. Dredge with caster sugar and cool on a wire rack. The biscuits may be frozen, well wrapped in polythene in a rigid container, for up to 3 months. Thaw for 1 – 2 hours at room temperature.

CHOCOLATE YULE LOG

Serves 10

3 eggs

75 g (3 oz) caster sugar

75 g (3 oz) plain flour, sifted twice

1 tbls hot water

1 tsp vanilla essence

For the filling and topping:

125 g (5 oz) sugar

6 tbls water

3 egg yolks

200 g (8 oz) unsalted butter, softened

100 g (4 oz) plain chocolate, melted and cooled

icing sugar

meringue mushrooms, to decorate

Heat the oven to 220°C, 425°F, Gas Mark 7. Whisk together the eggs and caster sugar until very thick and fluffy. Fold in the flour, water and vanilla essence, gently but thoroughly.

Pour into a 38 × 26 cm (15 × 10½ inch) Swiss roll tin. Bake in the oven for 8 to 10 minutes until golden.

Turn out on to a sheet of sugared greaseproof paper set on a damp teatowel. Trim the crusty edges. Roll up with the paper inside and leave to cool.

For the filling and topping, place the sugar and water in a small pan. Dissolve the sugar, stirring, over a low heat. When the sugar is dissolved, boil without stirring to 110°C, 230°F.

Whisk the egg yolks in a bowl and continue to whisk while pouring on the syrup in a thin stream. Whisk until thick and cooled. Gradually whisk in the butter and finally fold in the melted chocolate.

Unroll the cake and spread half the chocolate butter cream over it. Roll up neatly. Place on a silver board. Cut the end of the roll off at an angle and attach to one side of the roll to resemble a branch.

Cover the cake with the remaining chocolate cream and fork it to resemble bark. Chill until firm. Dust the cake with icing sugar. Attach the meringue mushrooms to the board and to the yule log.

Freeze the iced yule log in a rigid container for 3 months. Thaw for 3 hours at room temperature. Store the meringue mushrooms in an airtight container for up to 4 weeks. Decorate the log with the meringue mushrooms just before using.

LIGHT AND LOVELY CHRISTMAS CAKE

Makes 1 × 20 cm (8 inch) square cake

250 g (9 oz) plain flour

½ tsp ground cinnamon

250 g (9 oz) unsalted butter

225 g (8 oz) caster sugar

4 eggs, beaten

100 g (4 oz) ground almonds

175 g (6 oz) glacé cherries, halved, washed and dried

finely grated rind of 2 lemons

175 g (6 oz) blanched almonds, chopped

175 g (6 oz) crystallized pineapple, chopped

100 g (4 oz) dried apricots, chopped

3 tbls Cointreau

To decorate:

1.25 kg (2¼ lbs) marzipan

100 g (4 oz) apricot jam, sieved

Heat the oven to 160°C, 325°F, Gas Mark 3. Sieve together the flour and cinnamon. Cream the butter and sugar together and gradually beat in the eggs until the mixture is fluffy but stiff. Stir in all the other ingredients.

Turn into a greased, double-lined 20 cm (8 inch) square tin. Wrap the tin in thick brown paper and tie with string. Bake for 2–2¼ hours. Test with a skewer after 1¾ hours. Cool in the tin. Wrap and store for 4 weeks.

To decorate, reserve 225 g (8 oz) of the marzipan and set aside. Divide the remainder into 2 and roll half on an icing sugar-dusted surface to fit the top of the cake. Brush the cake top with jam and press on the marzipan.

Roll the other half to fit the sides of the cake. Brush the sides with jam and press on the marzipan.

Place the cake on a cake board. Using a knife, mark the top of the cake with lines to make a diamond or lattice pattern.

Knead the reserved marzipan until soft. Divide into four equal pieces. Roll three pieces into long ropes and plait together evenly. Press onto the cake, round the top edges, to form a rim.

Shape ivy leaves with some of the remaining marzipan. Roll thin tendrils between the fingers, and curl between the ivy leaves, arranged round the top of the cake, inside the plait.

Place the cake under a hot grill for just a few seconds to brown the marzipan lightly.

MERINGUE MUSHROOMS

1 egg white

50 g (2 oz) caster sugar

a little icing sugar

a little cocoa

Whisk the egg whites until very stiff. Gradually pour in half the sugar while continuing to whisk steadily. Whisk until stiff again. Fold in the remaining sugar.

Line a baking sheet with non-stick parchment. Pipe the meringue into an equal number of small buttons (for the caps) and stalks, using a large plain tube. Dry out overnight in an airing cupboard or in a very low oven for 1 to 2 hours. Cool.

Assemble the mushrooms by setting the caps on the stalks. Attach with a little uncooked meringue mixture. Mix the icing sugar and cocoa together and use to dust the mushrooms.

Using up turkey

Inevitably, there will be some turkey left over. Here are some ways of using turkey meat, and the turkey carcass afterwards.

TURKEY AU GRATIN

Serves 4
450 g (1 lb) cooked turkey, chopped
25 g (1 oz) butter
100 g (4 oz) blanched almonds
For the sauce:
25 g (1 oz) butter or margarine
25 g (1 oz) plain flour
600 ml (1 pint) milk
50 g (2 oz) Cheddar cheese, grated
1 garlic clove, crushed
salt and pepper
chopped fresh parsley
75 g (3 oz) brown breadcrumbs
Parmesan cheese, grated

Heat the oven to 160°C, 325°F, Gas Mark 3. Arrange the turkey in a shallow dish. Melt the butter and toss the almonds in it until golden. Sprinkle the nuts and butter over the turkey.

Melt the butter and stir in the flour. Add milk and simmer for 2 minutes. Add cheese and garlic, season to taste. Stir until the cheese has melted. Pour over the turkey. Dot with butter. Sprinkle the breadcrumbs and Parmesan on top. Cook in the the oven for 30 – 40 minutes. Garnish with parsley.

TURKEY CHART

When choosing your turkey, estimate how many servings you hope to get from it. Extra servings can be obtained by turning carcass pickings into a variety of dishes and the carcass itself will make stock for soups and sauces.

Oven-ready weight	Approx. No. of servings
2.25 – 3 kg (5 – 7 lb)	6 – 10
3.5 – 5.5 kg (8 – 12 lb)	10 – 15
6 – 7.5 kg (13 – 16 lb)	15 – 20
7.5 – 9 kg (17 – 20 lb)	20 – 30
9.5 – 11.25 kg (21 – 25 lb)	30 – 40
11.75 – 13.5 kg (26 – 30 lb)	40 – 50

COUNTRY–STYLE TURKEY PIE

Serves 6
50 g (2 oz) margarine
40 g (1½ oz) flour
750 ml (1¼ pints) milk
1½ chicken stock cubes, crumbled
salt
½ tsp Worcestershire sauce
1½ tbls dry sherry
3 drops Tabasco sauce
350 g (12 oz) cooked turkey, diced
175 g (6 oz) mushrooms, sliced
225 g (8 oz) carrots, cooked, sliced
225 g (8 oz) button onions, boiled
275 g (10 oz) packet puff pastry
beaten egg, to glaze
Parmesan cheese, grated

Heat the oven to 200°C, 400°F, Gas Mark 6. Melt the margarine in a pan, stir in the flour and cook for 1 minute. Stir in the milk very gradually and add the stock cubes, salt and Worcestershire sauce.

Bring to the boil, stirring with a wooden spoon, until the mixture thickens. Stir in the sherry and Tabasco sauce. Add the turkey, mushrooms, carrots, and drained onions, and heat through gently but thoroughly. Turn the mixture into a 1.75 litre (3 pint) pie dish.

Roll out the pastry and use to cover the dish, fluting the edges of the pastry against the rim. Make a small hole in the centre of the pastry to allow steam to escape. Decorate as desired with pastry trimmings – stars or holly leaves would be topical. Bake in the oven for about 20 minutes, until the pastry begins to brown.

Brush the top of the pie with beaten egg and sprinkle with cheese. Bake for a further 10 minutes until puffed up and brown.

Variation There are so many different ways to make use of this recipe. How about ringing the changes by using cooked chicken instead of turkey and adding 3 washed and sliced leeks and a small can of sweetcorn, but omitting the mushrooms. Alternatively, you could try adding 100 g (4 oz) dried, no soak apricots and 50 g (2 oz) chopped walnut pieces to the basic recipe for a more exotic flavour.

JELLIED TURKEY CONSOMMÉ

Serves 10

turkey carcass

1.75 litres (3 pints) water

1 bay leaf

1 can concentrated chicken or beef consommé

grated rind of 1 lemon

25 g (1 oz) powdered gelatine

salt and pepper

few drops Tabasco sauce

100 g (4 oz) shredded cooked turkey

1 lemon, sliced, for garnish

Place the turkey carcass in a large pan and cover with water. Add the bay leaf and simmer gently for 1½ – 2 hours.

Strain the soup into a clean pan and add the consommé, lemon rind and gelatine. Heat gently until the gelatine is dissolved. Season and add the Tabasco.

Leave in a cold place. As the soup begins to thicken, stir in the turkey. Leave to set.

To serve, spoon the jelly into bowls and top with a slice of lemon.

TURKEY AND ONION SOUP

Serves 6

turkey giblets and turkey bones

1.6 litres (2¾ pints) water

450 g (1 lb) onions, thinly sliced

65 g (2½ oz) margarine or butter

1 tbls plain flour

freshly ground black pepper

salt

2 bay leaves

To garnish:

6 slices French bread

75 g (3 oz) Cheddar cheese, grated

Put the giblets and bones in a pan of water. Bring to the boil, remove the scum, then cover and simmer for 1½ hours. Strain off the liquid. Remove some of the meat from the neck, chop finely and reserve (discard the remainder of the cooked giblets or use for a pie).

Fry the onions in melted fat until an even golden colour (avoid browning). Stir in the flour, then add the stock and bring to the boil. Season to taste and add the bay leaves. Cover and simmer for about 20 minutes. Discard the bay leaves. Add the chopped giblet meat. Continue simmering for 5 minutes.

To serve, ladle the soup into bowls. Float slices of bread with grated cheese toasted on the top of each bowl.

This soup will freeze in containers and keep for 2 – 4 weeks. Thaw in the container, heat and serve with the garnish.

Left to right: Country-style turkey pie; Turkey and onion soup; Turkey au gratin

THE CHRISTMAS BOOK
· CHRISTMAS EVE ·

The home is decorated with greenery, ribbons and glitter, the tree is trimmed and the parcels wrapped, while the first candles of Christmas are lit to greet close friends to this first feast of Christmas. Christmas Eve is a traditional English feast day so the meal must be special, but not outshine the Christmas Day celebration to come. The first course can be eaten away from the table, perhaps with one of the cups or punches on pages 18 – 21, while you enjoy the sound of carols. The other dishes make an exciting and festive meal to eat at table.

PLANNING CHART

Devilled chicken liver and bacon kebabs could be made the day before and left to marinate in the refrigerator overnight. Cook and serve immediately.

Crispy ricotta parcels can be made up to 1 month in advance and frozen. Thaw and reheat in the oven on baking sheets.

Rich beef and oyster pie filling can be made (without the oysters), and frozen up to 1 month ahead. On Christmas Eve, add the oysters and put on the pastry top. Chill in the refrigerator for up to 3 hours before cooking.

Creamed potatoes and celeriac can be made the day before, then covered and chilled. Reheat just before serving.

French buttered peas are simple and quick, so prepare them just before serving. This dish does not freeze or reheat well.

Tipsy tangerines can be made the day before and chilled overnight.

White chocolate mousse can be made the day before and chilled overnight, covered.

Almond wafers can be made a week or so before and stored in an airtight tin.

MENU

Devilled chicken liver
and bacon kebabs
Crispy ricotta parcels

Rich beef and oyster pie
Creamed potatoes
and celeriac
French Buttered peas

Tipsy tangerines
White chocolate mousse
Almond wafers

DEVILLED CHICKEN LIVER AND BACON KEBABS

Serves 8
350 g (12 oz) chicken livers
350 g (12 oz) streaky bacon, rinded
4 tsps Worcestershire sauce
4 tsps mushroom ketchup
2 tbls dried mustard
1 tsp lemon juice
1 tbls tomato purée
50 g (2 oz) butter, melted
watercress, to garnish

Cut the chicken livers into 2.5 cm (1 inch) pieces. Stretch the bacon rashers on a board with the back of a knife. Cut each rasher across in two and roll them up with the point of the knife.

Thread the liver pieces and bacon rolls alternately on to small skewers. Blend together the Worcestershire sauce, mushroom ketchup, mustard, lemon juice, tomato purée and butter. Place the kebabs close together in a deep dish and pour the sauce over them. Cover, chill and marinate them for up to 6 hours.

Place the kebabs on a rack and grill under a high heat for 5–10 minutes, basting with the remaining sauce as they cook. Serve hot, garnished with watercress.

Variation: Kebabs can be served as a main dish or a starter. For a main dish, accompany them with a green salad and French bread or on a bed of rice. Try using cubes of pork or lamb interspersed with onion and green pepper. You will find that the secret of delicious kebabs lies mostly in the marinade you use.

Simple marinade Combine 4 tbls oil, 4 tbls lemon juice, 2 tbls chopped parsley, 1 crushed garlic clove, salt and pepper.

Moroccan marinade Combine 1 small chopped onion, ½ tsp salt, 1 tsp ground cumin, ½ tsp black pepper, 4 tbls oil, and 1 tsp paprika for an extra-spicy flavour.

FRENCH BUTTERED PEAS
Serves 8

75 g (3 oz) butter

2 shallots or 6 spring onions, finely sliced

750 g (1½ lb) petit pois (frozen)

1 round lettuce, washed, dried, and shredded

1 tsp white sugar

salt and pepper

Melt the butter in a large shallow pan and fry the shallots for 4 – 5 minutes until golden.

Stir in the petit pois and cook, stirring for about 4 minutes. Finally add the lettuce, sugar and seasoning and cook for about 2 minutes, until the vegetables are tender.

Rich beef and oyster pie with Creamed potatoes and celeriac and French buttered peas; Tipsy tangerines

To make silver and green 'epergne', see page 50

CRISPY RICOTTA PARCELS
Serves 8

225 g (8 oz) ricotta cheese, softened

100 g (4 oz) frozen spinach, chopped and thawed

100 g (4 oz) smoked ham, finely chopped

¼ tsp ground nutmeg

freshly ground black pepper

8 sheets filo pastry (strudel leaves)

75 g (3 oz) butter, melted

Heat the oven to 220°C, 425°F, Gas Mark 7. Place the cheese in a bowl. Squeeze the spinach dry in a sieve and add to the cheese with the ham, nutmeg and ground pepper to taste. Mix them together well.

Lay out the sheets of pastry on a work surface and keep them moist under a damp teatowel. Taking out one sheet of pastry at a time, cut lengthwise into three equal strips and brush well with butter. Place a teaspoon of cheese at one end of each strip. Fold the pastry diagonally over the filling to enclose it in a triangle of pastry and continue to fold it over, working along the strip to finish with a neat triangular-shaped parcel of several layers of buttered pastry.

Brush with more butter and place on a baking sheet. Repeat the process with the remaining filling, pastry and butter. This will yield 24 small parcels. Bake in the oven for 8–10 minutes until golden brown. Serve hot.

Variation: Instead of using ricotta cheese you can mix equal quantities of curd and full fat soft cheese.

RICH BEEF AND OYSTER PIE
Serves 8

100 g (4 oz) butter
4 tbls oil
1.25 kg (2½ lb) braising or rump steak, trimmed
225 g (8 oz) ox kidney, trimmed
75 g (3 oz) plain flour
salt and pepper
2 large onions, sliced
2 sticks celery, chopped
225 g (8 oz) button mushrooms, halved
1 bouquet garni
300 ml (½ pint) beef stock
300 ml (½ pint) red wine
18 fresh oysters (optional)
350 g (12 oz) puff pastry, thawed if frozen
beaten egg, to glaze

Heat the butter and oil in a large, flameproof casserole. Cut the meats into 2.5 cm (1 inch) cubes. Season the flour with plenty of salt and pepper and toss the meats in the flour. Fry the meat in the hot butter and oil, in batches, to brown on all sides. Remove the meat. Add the onion and celery and fry for 3 minutes.

Devilled chicken liver and bacon kebabs; Crispy ricotta parcels

Return the meat to the pan with any left-over seasoned flour and stir in the mushrooms and bouquet garni. Add the stock and wine and bring to the boil. Cover and simmer for 1½–2 hours or until tender. If there is too much liquid, reduce it by pouring some into a pan and boiling rapidly, returning the reduced liquid to the dish.

Allow the meat to cool and skim off any fat. Push a short-bladed knife under the hinge of the oyster shells to prize them apart and remove the oyster, taking care not to spill the liquor. Stir the oysters and their liquor into the meat. Transfer the filling to a 1.2 litre (2 pint) pie dish.

Heat the oven to 220°C, 425°F, Gas Mark 7. Roll out the pastry on a floured surface to 5 cm (2 inch) larger than the top of the pie dish. Trim 2.5 cm (1 inch) from round the edge of the pastry and attach this to the wetted rim of the pie dish. Brush with water. Lay the pastry top on the pie. Trim round and 'knock up' the edge with the back of a knife. Make a decorative pattern on the crust. Make a slit in the pastry for the steam to escape. Use the trimmings to decorate the pie (holly leaf shapes would be topical). Brush the pastry with beaten egg. Bake in the oven for 30–40 minutes until the pastry is well-risen and golden brown.

CREAMED POTATOES AND CELERIAC
Serves 8

1 kg (2 lb) potatoes, sliced
1 large celeriac, sliced
50 g (2 oz) butter
150 ml (¼ pint) soured cream or yoghurt
freshly ground black pepper
To garnish:
toasted flaked almonds
parsley sprig

Boil the potatoes and the celeriac separately in salted water until tender. Purée the vegetables in a food processor or through a sieve. Cut the butter into small pieces and stir into the hot purée. Blend in the soured cream with plenty of freshly ground black pepper.

Put into a dish and serve garnished with toasted flaked almonds and a sprig of parsley. (This dish is ideal for making in advance and may be reheated just before serving in a bowl set over boiling water, or in a microwave oven.)

TIPSY TANGERINES
Serves 8

8 large tangerines
75 g (3 oz unsalted butter)
175 g (6 oz) caster sugar
300 ml (½ pint) orange juice
juice and grated rind of 1 lemon
4 tbls Cointreau (or other orange liqueur)
bay leaves, to garnish

Carefully peel the tangerines so that the segments remain attached. Peel off as much pith as possible. Place the fruit in a shallow bowl.

Place the butter and sugar in a pan and heat gently until the sugar dissolves and the mixture becomes golden brown.

Remove the pan from the heat and stir in the orange juice. Add the lemon rind and juice. Cook gently, stirring, until a smooth sauce develops. Bubble the sauce to thicken it.

Warm the Cointreau in a metal ladle, pour it over the sauce and ignite. Pour the sauce over the fruit. Allow to cool, basting the fruit frequently. Chill.

Serve decorated with bay leaves.

WHITE CHOCOLATE MOUSSE

Serves 8

225 g (8 oz) white chocolate, grated
25 g (1 oz) unsalted butter
4 eggs, separated
2 tsps gelatine
3 tbls water
2 tbls white rum
150 ml (¼ pint) double cream, lightly whipped
dark chocolate, to decorate

Place the chocolate in a large jug with the butter, and stand it in a bowl of hot (not boiling) water. Stir until the chocolate and butter are melted and smooth.

Remove the jug from the water and stir in the 4 egg yolks. Sprinkle the gelatine over the water in a small bowl over a pan of hot water and stir until dissolved. Cool, and add the rum. Pour into the melted chocolate mixture and stir until blended. Whisk the egg whites until stiff. Fold the cream into the chocolate, followed by the egg whites.

Pour into small dessert glasses and allow to set. Serve decorated with dark chocolate.

Variation: For marbled chocolate mousse, make the mousse as above. Pour into serving glasses or one large bowl. Scatter 50 g (2 oz) of melted dark chocolate in large drops over the surface of the mousse. Swirl a skewer through the drops to make a marbled effect.

You may want to make this pudding in the spring or summer. As an alternative decoration, crystallized violets are lovely. Dip or paint the flowers in egg white and coat with caster sugar. Set aside in a warm place to set and then store them in airtight containers until they are required.

ALMOND WAFERS

Makes 16

2 egg whites
100 g (4 oz) caster sugar
50 g (2 oz) plain flour, sifted
50 g (2 oz) butter, melted and cooled
few drops of almond essence

Heat the oven to 190°C, 375°F, Gas Mark 5. Line a baking sheet with non-stick baking parchment. Beat the egg whites

White chocolate mousse with Almond wafers

and sugar together in a bowl with a wooden spoon until the mixture is smooth. Stir in the flour and butter and then fold in the almond essence. Spread the wafer mixture thinly on the baking sheets in either rounds or rectangles about 7.5 cm (3 inches) across.

Bake in the oven for approximately 5 minutes or until the wafers are just beginning to turn a light golden brown around the edges.

Slide the baking parchment off the baking sheet to prevent the wafers cooking further. Slip a palette knife under the wafers to remove them from the paper and roll each round the handle of a wooden spoon. Slide them off and leave until set. Repeat with the remaining mixture (do not attempt to do them all at once on several baking sheets as you will not have time to roll them all while they are still hot).

Serve the wafers with the Tipsy tangerines and with the White chocolate mousse.

Variation: Dip the ends of the rolled wafers in melted chocolate. Allow to set on a wire rack before serving. You can also vary the chocolate decoration as you like – try dipping both ends in the chocolate, piping 'scribbles' all over the wafers, or alternatively using a mixture of dark and white chocolate to create a ripple or marbled effect.

Holly, ivy and fir make delightful decorations for the Christmas table – but they are poisonous. Take great care they do not come into contact with the food and make sure children do not mistake them for edibles!

· THE FESTIVE BOWL ·

Drinks for your Christmas celebrations need to be planned as carefully as the festive foods. It adds to the festive feeling if guests are offered a traditional hot punch or grog on arrival and when leaving. Cups are a delicious alternative during a party.

Some people prefer not to drink alcohol, particularly if they are driving home afterwards, but this need not mean their drinks are limited to straight fruit drinks or tonic water. Interesting 'pussy-foots' are included in the recipes so that everyone can have a special celebration drink.

Punches

Punch is traditionally served from a large bowl with a ladle. Victorian wash bowls make charming punch bowls, or alternatively a large mixing bowl can be used; arrange greenery around the sides to mask the utilitarian appearance. If you do not have a bowl of suitable size, serve from a large cooking pot or saucepan. Punch should be served freshly made and hot. If the mixture is re-heated, you risk the alcoholic content evaporating and the punch loses its 'kick'.

Do not be tempted to serve guests with more than one – or two – punch drinks. Most punches are very palatable and easy to drink, but as some recipes have a mixture of alcoholic drinks in them it is easy to give your guests more than is good for them!

HEARTWARMER
Serves 12

200 ml (7 fl oz) red grape juice

225 g (8 oz) brown sugar

350 ml (12 fl oz) dark rum

1.5 litres (2½ pints) dry white wine

450 ml (¾ pint) red wine

Warm the grape juice with the brown sugar until the sugar has completely dissolved. Stir in the rum and put aside. Put the white wine and red wine together in a saucepan and cook until they are hot but not boiling. Add the rum and grape juice mixture and stir together. Serve hot.

CHRISTMAS PUNCH
Serves 8

10 sugar lumps

2 large oranges

8 cloves

1 tsp cinnamon

1 tsp ground nutmeg

150 ml (¼ pint) water

thinly peeled rind and juice of 2 lemons

1.2 litres (2 pints) dry cider

150 ml (¼ pint) rum or brandy

Rub the sugar cubes over the oranges to absorb the zest. Squeeze the juice from one orange and put into the pan with the sugar. Cut the second orange into eighths. Push a clove into the peel of each segment. Add to the juice and sugar, sprinkle on the spices and stir. Leave to marinate for 15 minutes.

Add the water, lemon rind and juice. Heat gently without stirring until the sugar dissolves, then add the cider. Continue cooking until hot. Add the rum or brandy and serve hot.

BISHOP
Serves 12

3 oranges

24 cloves

½ bottle of inexpensive port

1 tbls clear honey

2 tbls brandy, warmed

Heat the oven to 180°C, 350°F, Gas Mark 4. Stud two of the oranges with cloves and bake in a dish in the oven until the oranges begin to go soft and slightly brown (about 15 minutes).

Heat the port and honey together in a saucepan and add one of the cooked oranges. Simmer for about 15 minutes. Put the second baked orange into a ladle or a large spoon and pour the brandy over it. Set the orange alight and, while it is still burning, lower it into the port. Slice the third orange thinly and add to the punch. Serve hot in glasses, making sure there is a slice of orange in each glass.

The word 'punch' comes from an Indian word for 'five' and is associated with the five basic ingredients – sugar, water, spirits, spices and lemon juice. The heavy drinking of the early eighteenth century became unfashionable in 'society' and punches and toddies, where the spirits were diluted, became more popular.

PEAR PUNCH

Mix 2 × 1 litre (1¾ pints) bottles of pear cider with 1 tsp ground ginger, ½ tsp cinnamon, ½ tsp ground cloves. Boil, then simmer for a few minutes and remove from the heat. Add a dash of Worcestershire sauce. Slice whole oranges and eating apples thinly, pour the punch over the fruit and serve.

Left to right: Cider cup; Bishop; Spicy fruit punch

Left to right: Mulled ale;
Mulled claret; Egg nog;
Bottom left: Florentines
(see page 45)

Mulled drinks

Mulls were traditionally mixed at the fireside and heated with a red-hot poker. Nowadays open fires are less common but we can still enjoy these warming drinks.

MULLED ALE

Serves 10

1.2 litre (2 pints) brown ale
150 ml (¼ pint) rum or brandy
3 tbls brown sugar
6 cloves
1 tsp ground ginger
pinch of ground nutmeg and cinnamon
thinly peeled rind and juice of 1 lemon
thinly peeled rind and juice of 1 orange
600 ml (1 pint) water
orange slice, to decorate

Put all ingredients except the orange slice into a large pan. Bring slowly to a boil, stirring all the time to dissolve the sugar. Turn off the heat and leave to stand for a few minutes. Strain into a warmed jug and serve, with a slice of orange on top.

MULLED CLARET

Serves 9

1 bottle claret
¼ bottle inexpensive port
600 ml (1 pint) boiling water
brown or white sugar to taste
pinch of ground nutmeg
cinnamon stick

Heat the claret and port together in a saucepan, pour in the water and stir. Add the sugar and nutmeg and serve hot, with a stick of cinnamon.

Grogs

A hot grog, served on a cold night, warms the heart and makes the going home easier. Grogs can be a simple mixture of whisky or rum with hot water, perhaps flavoured with a little honey or brown sugar. This Goodnight grog also uses tea.

GOODNIGHT GROG

Serves 8

900 ml (1½ pints) Indian tea, strained
300 ml (½ pint) dark rum or whisky
2 tbls brown sugar or 50 g (2 oz) clear honey
5 cm (2 inch) cinnamon stick
pinch of mixed spice

Put the tea into a saucepan with the rum or whisky, sugar or honey, the cinnamon stick and the spice. Heat gently, stirring constantly. Leave the grog to stand for a few minutes and then remove the cinnamon stick. Serve warm to hot in handled glasses or pretty mugs.

GINGER SNAP

Serves 4

300 ml (½ pint) water
275 ml (9 fl oz) ginger wine
2 tbls lime juice
1 tbls brown sugar
pinch of ground nutmeg

Heat the water to boiling and pour over the other ingredients in a bowl or jug. Stir until the sugar dissolves. Serve hot.

EGG NOG

Egg Nog is Dutch in origin and makes a different kind of drink to serve for a morning drinks party.

Serves 8-10

10 egg yolks
100 g (4 oz) caster sugar
475 ml (16 fl oz) brandy

Beat the egg yolks with the sugar until thick and light coloured and all the sugar is dissolved. Fold in the brandy. Serve immediately in small glasses.

SPARKLING COCKTAIL

Serves 1

Into a large wineglass put 1 small sugar cube, 2 drops of bitters and 1 tbls of brandy. Leave until the sugar has dissolved. To serve, top up with dry sparkling white wine.

CLARET CUP

Serves 8

thinly peeled rind of 1 lemon
90 ml (3 fl oz) white rum
1 miniature bottle of orange-flavoured liqueur
2 bottles claret
3 bottles ginger ale

Marinate the lemon peel in the rum and liqueur for about 2 hours. To serve, pour over the claret and ginger ale and stir. Chill with ice cubes.

CIDER CUP

Serves 8

1 litre (1¾ pints) bottle dry cider
1 litre (1¾ pints) bottle soda water
1 wineglass of brandy
1 tbls lemon juice
25 g (1 oz) sugar (optional)
To decorate:
thin strips of cucumber peel
thin strips of lemon rind

Chill the cider and soda. Pour into a chilled bowl with the brandy and lemon juice and stir well. If desired, add sugar to sweeten. Decorate with cucumber and lemon peel strips and serve in chilled glasses.

LOVING CUP

Serves 12

8 sugar cubes
2 lemons
½ bottle medium sweet or sweet sherry
¼ bottle brandy
1 bottle dry sparkling white wine

Rub the sugar cubes over the lemons to absorb the zest. Peel the lemons thinly and remove as much of the pith as possible. Slice the lemons thinly and put aside.

Put the lemon peel, sherry and brandy and sugar cubes in a jug and stir until the sugar is dissolved. Chill for about 30 minutes. Pour in the wine just before serving and float the lemon slices on top.

SPICY FRUIT PUNCH

600 ml (1 pint) orange juice
600 ml (1 pint) apple juice
150 ml (¼ pint) water
½ tsp ground ginger
½ tsp mixed spice
brown or white sugar to taste (optional)
1 apple, thinly sliced, to decorate

Place the juices, water and spices in a saucepan and bring gently to the boil, stirring in sugar to taste. Simmer for 5 minutes.

Pour into a warmed punch bowl and serve with slices of apple on top. You can also serve this drink chilled for a summer party.

Syrups

Flavoured syrup makes a delicious base for cups and for soft drinks. Make it before Christmas and bottle it ready for use. Try experimenting with different flavours so you have a wide selection of drinks to offer friends.

ORANGE SYRUP

thinly peeled rind and juice of 3 large oranges
900 ml (1½ pints) water
1 kg (2 lb) granulated sugar
1 tbls citric acid

Place the orange peel in a pan with the water and sugar. Heat gently, stirring until all the sugar is dissolved. Bring to the boil and boil for 10 minutes. Remove from the heat and leave to stand overnight.

The next day, stir in the orange juice and citric acid. Strain and pour the syrup into bottles. Seal tightly with a cork and store for up to 3 months.

Variations:

Lemon syrup is made in the same way, or a mixture of oranges and lemons makes an interesting flavour.

Ginger lemon Slice 25 g (1 oz) of ginger root into the syrup before boiling.

Lemon syrup drinks For a pleasantly soothing nightcap, dilute lemon syrup with hot water and add a pinch each of ground cloves, cinnamon and allspice.

· CHRISTMAS DAY ·

Christmas Day is so full of excitement, with the opening of presents and the arrival of guests, that it is difficult for the hostess to keep to any kind of schedule. Planning and cooking during the weeks before Christmas will ensure that a lot of the food needs only heating through to make a feast to remember. The schedule on this page will help you to achieve this – adjust the times for an evening meal.

Lay the party table as early in the day as possible, so that you can add the final, decorative touches in odd moments – and leave yourself time also to enjoy your guests and family.

CHRISTMAS FEAST COUNT-DOWN

Christmas Eve: Prepare Watercress creams, Chocolate truffles.

Thaw Stuffings, Cranberry sauce, Baby onions and chestnuts, Strawberry mousse cake.

Peel potatoes, parsnips, sprouts and carrots. Keep the potatoes in cold water to prevent browning and wrap the other vegetables in polythene bags and chill in the refrigerator.

Christmas Day: 9.00 am Heat the oven to 160°C, 325°F, Gas Mark 3. Stuff and prepare the 5.4 kg/12 lb turkey, wrap in foil and put in the oven.

11.00 am Begin steaming the Christmas pudding. Baste the turkey.

12.00 am Put the potatoes and parsnips to roast on top shelf. Decorate the Strawberry mousse cake.

12.15 pm Arrange Watercress creams on serving plates. Garnish, cover with film and chill.

12.30 pm Baste the turkey. Remove the foil and raise the oven to 200°C, 400°F, Gas Mark 6. Prepare the garnishes.

12.45 pm Put the chipolatas and bacon rolls in the oven.

1.00 pm Test the turkey and remove to a serving dish if ready. Cover with foil to keep warm. Heat the Casseroled onions and chestnuts, and the Cranberry sauce.

Make gravy, pour into a gravy boat and keep warm. If you are having red wine with the turkey, open the bottle to allow the wine to 'breathe'.

1.15 pm Cook the Buttered sprouts with almonds and the Orange-glazed carrots. Place the vegetables in serving dishes and keep warm. Make Brandy Sabayon Sauce and keep warm. Carve the turkey.

1.30 pm Serve the first course.

WATERCRESS CREAMS

Serves 6—8
450 ml (¾ pint) strongly flavoured chicken or vegetable stock
4 bunches watercress, trimmed
20 g (¾ oz) powdered gelatine
3 tbls water (or stock)
freshly ground black pepper
finely grated rind of ½ lemon
1 tsp lemon juice
150 ml (¼ pint) soured cream or yoghurt
100 g (4 oz) curd or full fat soft cheese
To garnish:
watercress sprigs
lemon twists

Bring the stock to the boil, add the watercress and simmer gently for 4 minutes. Blend the watercress and stock together in a liquidizer until smooth. Sprinkle the gelatine over the water in a bowl, set it over a pan of hot water and stir until the gelatine is completely dissolved. Allow the gelatine to cool, then blend into the watercress purée with the pepper, lemon rind and juice. Finally, add the soured cream or yoghurt and curd or full fat soft cheese. Check the seasoning and adjust if necessary.

Pour the purée into a bowl and allow to set in the refrigerator for 1 hour. Serve the watercress cream in scoops on plates, garnished with sprigs of watercress and lemon twists. Serve with Melba toast.

Variation: You might like to pour the purée into individual ramekins to set. Try serving garnished with twists or slices of lime instead of lemon.

ROAST POTATOES

Peel potatoes and cut them to approximately similar sizes. Parboil in salted water, then put into a small roasting pan. Dot with pieces of cooking fat, season and place in the oven with the turkey, until browned.

WINE GRAVY
Makes 600 ml (1 pint)

2 tbls plain flour

150 ml (¼ pint) full-bodied red wine

450 ml (¾ pint) giblet stock

few drops of gravy browning

salt and pepper (optional)

2 tbls redcurrant jelly

Pour all but 1 tbls of fat from the roasting tin. Stir in the flour. Blend in the wine, stock and gravy browning and season if desired. Stir in the redcurrant jelly. Cook, stirring, for 5 minutes, then pour into a gravy boat.

MENU

Watercress Creams

Roast Turkey with two stuffings

Wine gravy, Cranberry Sauce
Chipolata sausages in bacon rolls
Roast potatoes, Roast parsnips
Buttered sprouts with almonds
Casseroled baby onions and chestnuts
Orange-glazed carrots

Christmas Pudding with
Brandy Sabayon sauce
Strawberry Mousse Cake

ROAST PARSNIPS

Peel, quarter and slice the parsnips, then cook in boiling, salted water for 5 minutes. Drain and place in a small roasting pan. Pour over melted fat, season, and roast for approximately ¾ hour. Garnish with chopped parsley.

ORANGE-GLAZED CARROTS

Peel or scrape young carrots and quarter them lengthwise. Melt a little butter in a pan, add the carrots and season. Add a pinch of sugar and just enough water to cover. Cook slowly, uncovered. As the water evaporates, add 2 tbls orange juice. Cook until the carrots are soft and the liquid has evaporated, leaving a slight glaze. Serve with a knob of butter, and sprinkle with chopped parsley.

Clockwise from top: Roast potatoes, Roast parsnips and Orange-glazed carrots; Rich and boozy Christmas pudding; Brandy Sabayon sauce; Watercress creams; Roast turkey with Wine Gravy, Pecan stuffing, Sweetcorn and honey stuffing, Chipolata sausages in bacon rolls, Buttered sprouts and Cranberry sauce; Casseroled baby onions and chestnuts.

To make traditional yule log table decoration, see page 50.

— 23 —

BUTTERED SPROUTS WITH ALMONDS

Serves 6

50 g (2 oz) butter

50 g (2 oz) flaked almonds

1 kg (2 lb) brussels sprouts, trimmed

Melt the butter in a small pan until foaming. Add the almonds and fry until golden brown but do not allow the butter to burn.

Cook the sprouts in boiling water until just tender. Drain. Return to a clean pan with the butter and almonds and toss to coat. Serve immediately.

ROAST TURKEY

Serves 8 – 12

5.4 kg (12 lb) turkey

50 g (2 oz) dripping or butter, melted

salt and pepper

Heat the oven to 160°C, 325°F, Gas Mark 3. Wash the turkey and pat dry with kitchen paper. Spoon the stuffings into the neck and body cavity of the turkey. Sew up both openings with trussing string, or secure with skewers. Weigh the stuffed bird and calculate the cooking time at 15 minutes per 450 g (1 lb), plus 15 minutes. Brush with dripping and season. Place on a rack in a roasting tin and cover with foil. Roast for calculated time; baste and turn occasionally. Remove foil for last 15 minutes. To test, pierce thigh with a skewer; it is done when the juices run clear.

Remove from the oven and transfer to a heated serving plate. Remove the string or skewers and keep warm by covering with a piece of foil.

SWEETCORN AND HONEY STUFFING

Makes sufficient to stuff 1 cavity of a 5.4 kg (12 lb) bird

200 g (7 oz) can of sweetcorn, drained

grated rind and juice of 1 lemon

2 tbls clear honey

1 dessert apple, grated

100 g (4 oz) fresh brown breadcrumbs

1 egg yolk

freshly ground black pepper, sea salt

Combine all the ingredients in a bowl and season to taste. The mixture should be moist and stick together without being 'sloppy'.

PECAN STUFFING

Makes sufficient to stuff 1 cavity of a 5.4 kg (12 lb) bird

heart and liver from turkey (or chicken)

50 g (2 oz) fresh breadcrumbs

50 g (2 oz) shelled pecan nuts, finely chopped

1 egg, hardboiled and chopped

pinch each of nutmeg, ground mace, dried thyme

1 tbls chopped fresh parsley

pinch of celery salt

40 g (1½ oz) butter

50 g (2 oz) mushrooms, wiped and finely chopped

1 small onion, peeled and chopped

2 tbls sherry

freshly ground black pepper

Put the meat in a pan, cover with water and cook for 10 minutes. Drain, chop finely, and cool. Put the meat in a bowl and add the breadcrumbs, nuts, egg, spices, herbs and celery salt. Melt the butter in a pan, sauté the mushrooms and onion until soft. Stir into the meat, add sherry and season.

RICH AND BOOZY CHRISTMAS PUDDING

Serves 8 (1 large pudding)

175 g (6 oz) currants

175 g (6 oz) raisins

100 g (4 oz) sultanas

juice and grated rind of ½ orange

grated rind of ½ lemon

175 g (6 oz) fresh brown breadcrumbs

50 g (2 oz) blanched almonds, chopped

½ tsp freshly grated nutmeg

½ tsp ground cinnamon

50 g (2 oz) soft dark brown sugar

2 eggs, beaten

2 tbls brandy

2 tbls port

2 tbls rum

100 g (4 oz unsalted butter, melted and cooled

holly sprig, to decorate

Mix together the dried fruit, orange and lemon rind, breadcrumbs, nuts, spices, and sugar. Whisk together the orange juice, eggs, spirits and melted butter. Stir the two mixtures together and mix well.

Turn into a 1.2 litre (2 pint) buttered pudding basin. Leave to stand for 1 hour.

Cover the basin with doubled, greased, greaseproof paper, pleating the edges to allow for expansion. Then cover with foil, pleating the edges to secure. Tie securely with string. Steam the pudding for 7 hours, adding boiling water to the steamer or saucepan as necessary. If you are using a pressure cooker, place the basin on a trivet and add 2 litres (3½ pints) of boiling

CASSEROLED BABY ONIONS AND CHESTNUTS

Serves 6

450 g (1 lb) chestnuts

50 g (2 oz) butter

450 g (2 oz) baby onions

300 ml (½ pint) chicken stock

1 tsp caster sugar

freshly ground black pepper

Heat the oven to 180°C, 350°F, Gas Mark 4. Make a slit in the skin of each chestnut and boil them for 5 minutes. Peel the chestnuts while warm, removing the outer and inner skin. Set aside.

Melt the butter in a small flameproof casserole dish. Add the onions and cook for 3 minutes without browning. Pour in the stock, cover and bake in the oven for 30 minutes until tender. Add the chestnuts, sugar and pepper and simmer on the hob, uncovered, until the liquid is reduced to a glaze. Serve hot.

BRANDY SABAYON SAUCE
Serves 6–8

4 egg yolks

4 tbls caster sugar

4 tbls brandy

juice and grated rind of ½ lemon

6 tbls orange juice

shredded peel, to garnish

Whisk the egg yolks and sugar together in a bowl over a pan of hot water until light and frothy. Whisking continuously, gradually pour in the brandy, lemon juice and rind, and the orange juice. Continue whisking over the hot water until the sauce is thick and fluffy. Serve warm with Christmas pudding. Garnish with shredded orange peel.

water. Fit the lid and steam without pressure for 30 minutes. Bring to high pressure and cook for 3 hours. Reduce the pressure slowly.

When cooked, allow to cool completely. Replace the paper and foil with fresh wrappings. Store in a cool, dry place, or freeze. Use within 1 year.

To reheat, steam for 2½ hours, cook at high pressure for 30 minutes in a pressure cooker and reduce the pressure slowly, or microwave for 4–6 minutes and allow to stand for 5 minutes. Remove the papers and turn out on to a hot serving dish. Decorate with a sprig of holly to serve.

STRAWBERRY MOUSSE CAKE

Serves 6–8
2 eggs
50 g (2 oz) caster sugar
50 g (2 oz) plain flour
few drops of almond essence
2 tsps boiling water
2 tbls orange juice
2 tbls marsala or sweet sherry
For the mousse:
50 g (2 oz) cottage cheese, sieved
50 g (2 oz) full fat soft cheese, softened
50 g (2 oz) caster sugar
1 egg, separated
juice and finely grated rind of ½ lemon
175 g (6 oz) frozen strawberries
1 tbls gelatine
3 tbls water
150 ml (¼ pint) double or whipping cream, whipped
sliced strawberries to decorate

Heat the oven to 220°C, 425°F, Gas Mark 7. Whisk the eggs and sugar together in a bowl over a pan of hot water until very thick and light. The whisk should leave a trail in the mixture for several seconds.

Sift the flour three times and sprinkle over the surface of the egg mixture. Gently fold in the almond essence and boiling water. Pour into a greased, lined Swiss roll tin. Bake in the oven for 8–10 minutes or until golden and risen. Turn out on to a wire rack to cool.

Line the base and ends of a 1 kg (2 lb) loaf tin with greaseproof paper. Trim one half of the cooked sponge to fit the base of the loaf tin. Blend the orange juice and Marsala and sprinkle half of it over the sponge in the tin.

For the mousse, beat together the cheeses, sugar and egg yolk. Stir in the lemon rind and juice. Press the strawberries through a sieve on to the cheese mixture and stir well.

Sprinkle the gelatine over the water in a small bowl and stir well until completely dissolved over a pan of hot water. Cool thoroughly and blend into the mousse. Beat the egg white until stiff. Reserving 4–5 tablespoons of the whipped cream, fold the remaining cream into the mousse. Finally, fold in the beaten egg white.

Pour the mousse over the sponge in the tin. Chill until it begins to set. Trim the remaining piece of sponge to fit on top of the mousse in the loaf tin. Sprinkle with the remaining orange juice and marsala and place the cake on top of the mousse, pressing down. Chill, and allow to set firm.

To serve: run a knife round the mousse and turn out onto a serving plate. Remove the paper and pipe the reserved cream down the centre. Decorate with slices of strawberry.

This cake may be made ahead of time and frozen for up to one month. Thaw in the refrigerator overnight.

Truffles (see page 45); Strawberry mousse cake

· VEGETARIAN CHRISTMAS ·

As all vegetarians know, you do not need to use animal products to create mouth-watering, festive foods. This delicious feast starts with an unusual fruit and vegetable soup; the highlight of the menu is a Cashew nut roll, an exciting and tasty dish which vegetarians and meat-eaters alike will enjoy. Non-vegetarians who share your Christmas day will soon realise that Christmas dinner does not have to include the traditional turkey or goose.

For an extra healthy Christmas meal, you may like to make the mince pies using wholemeal flour.

Make the most of the wide variety of nuts available at this time of the year and scatter the house with bowls of them, decoratively arranged with greenery.

PLANNING AHEAD

Tomato and raspberry soup This can be made in advance and frozen for up to 2 months. Thaw at room temperature and reheat gently, stirring.

Cashew nut roll The roll must be freshly made. The filling can be made in advance and frozen, excluding the cashew nuts, which are added at the final stage. Freeze for one month only.

Potato and leek bake Cook and serve fresh.

Courgettes with orange This dish is best cooked and served fresh, but you can make it in advance and freeze it for 1 month.

Apricot and almond pudding Cool the pudding after cooking and re-cover it with fresh greaseproof paper and foil. Freeze for up to 6 months.

Vegetarian mince pies Make these in the usual way, but do not bake. Freeze, then remove from the tins and transfer to containers. Freeze up to 1 month.

Cumberland rum butter This can be made 2-3 weeks in advance and kept in covered pots in refrigerator.

MENU

Tomato and Raspberry Soup

•

Cashew nut roll
Potato and leek bake
Courgettes with orange

——

Apricot and almond pudding
Mince pies
(vegetarian mincemeat)
Cumberland rum butter

TOMATO AND RASPBERRY SOUP

Serves 6
2 tbls vegetable oil
1 onion, chopped
2 sticks celery, chopped
2 small carrots, chopped
2 × 397 g (14 oz) can chopped tomatoes
300 ml (½ pint) vegetable stock
freshly ground black pepper
450 g (1 lb) frozen raspberries, defrosted and sieved
2 tsps lemon juice
2 tsps caster sugar (optional)
To garnish:
mint sprigs
150 g (5 oz) carton natural yoghurt

Heat the oil in a large pan. Fry the onion, celery and carrots for 5 minutes until softened but not browned.

Add the tomatoes and stock and season with pepper. Bring to the boil, then allow to simmer for 15 minutes.

Add raspberry purée, lemon juice, and sugar if desired, and check the seasoning. Purée in a blender and warm through before serving.

Garnish with mint and a spoonful of yoghurt, swirled with a cocktail stick.

COURGETTES WITH ORANGE

Serves 6
750 g (1½ lb) courgettes, sliced
grated rind and juice of 2 oranges
freshly ground black pepper
25 g (1 oz) butter

Place the courgettes and orange rind with the juice in a small pan. Cover tightly and simmer for about 4 minutes until the courgettes are tender.

Add the pepper and butter and toss until the courgettes are well coated. Serve hot.

VEGETARIAN MINCEMEAT

Makes 1.5 kg (3½ lb)

200 ml (7 fl oz) dry cider

150 g (6 oz) brown sugar

1 kg (2 lb) cooking apples, cored and chopped

1 tsp ground mixed spice

1 nutmeg, grated

225 g (8 oz) seedless raisins

100 g (4 oz) sultanas

100 g (4 oz) currants

50 g (2 oz) mixed peel

50 g (2 oz) flaked almonds

grated rind and juice of 1 small orange

grated rind and juice of 1 lemon

2 tbls brandy

Heat the cider and sugar together until the sugar has dissolved. Stir in the remaining ingredients, except the brandy. Cover and simmer for 45 minutes until the liquid has been absorbed.

Stir in the brandy. Spoon into clean, warmed jars. Seal and store in a cool place for up to 6 months. Once opened, store in the refrigerator.

CUMBERLAND RUM BUTTER

Serves 6–8

100 g (4 oz) unsalted butter

225 g (8 oz) soft brown sugar

¼ tsp ground nutmeg

pinch of ground cinnamon

45 ml (1½ fl oz) rum

Cream the butter, adding the sugar a little at a time, and mix in the spices. Add the rum very gradually or the mixture may curdle. The rum butter can be kept in small covered pots in the refrigerator for 2–3 weeks.

Clockwise from top: Mince pies (see page 9) with Vegetarian mincemeat; Cumberland rum butter; Apricot and almond pudding; Cashew nut roll with Courgettes with orange; Tomato and raspberry soup; Potato and leek bake

CASHEW NUT ROLL

Serves 6

40 g (1½ oz) butter

40 g (1½ oz) flour

250 ml (8 fl oz) milk

4 small eggs, separated

100 g (4 oz) cashew nuts, lightly toasted and coarsely ground

freshly ground black pepper

For the filling:

450 g (1 lb) tomatoes, skinned

2 sticks celery, chopped

2 shallots, chopped

½ tsp oregano

2 tbls tomato purée

100 g (4 oz) cashew nuts, lightly toasted and coarsely chopped

To garnish:

finely grated Parmesan cheese

coriander leaves

Heat the oven to 190°C, 375°F, Gas Mark 5. Melt the butter in a small pan. Stir in the flour and cook for 1 minute. Gradually blend in the milk, and cook until the mixture thickens. Remove from the heat and stir in the egg yolks and ground cashew nuts. Season with black pepper.

Whisk the egg whites stiffly and stir a spoonful of egg white into the sauce mixture. Fold in the remaining egg whites. Spread the mixture in a greased and lined 23 × 33 cm (9 × 13 inch) Swiss roll tin. Bake in the oven for 15–20 minutes until set and golden.

Meanwhile, make the filling. Place the tomatoes, celery, shallots, oregano and tomato purée in a pan and simmer gently until thick and pulpy. Stir in the cashew nuts, reserving a few for garnish.

Turn out the cooked roll on to a hot, clean, damp tea towel, covered with a sheet of greaseproof paper. Trim the edges. Spread the filling over the roll and roll up from a short side, using the tea towel to help you to roll.

Sprinkle with Parmesan cheese and cashew nuts. Serve hot in slices, garnished with coriander leaves.

Variation: For an extra zing, you could spice up the tomato filling by adding 1 tsp of sweet chilli sauce or a few drops of Tabasco sauce, but be careful when adding this as it is extremely powerful!

POTATO AND LEEK BAKE

Serves 6

1.25 kg (2½ lbs) potatoes

450 g (1 lb) leeks, trimmed and sliced

freshly ground black pepper

142 ml (5 fl oz) carton single cream

50 g (2 oz) Cheddar cheese, grated

25 g (1 oz) fresh breadcrumbs

parsley sprigs, to garnish

Heat the oven to 190°C, 375°F, Gas Mark 5. Parboil the potatoes for 3 minutes. Drain and slice. Place the leeks in a greased ovenproof dish and season with pepper. Arrange the potatoes on the top and pour the cream over. Cover with foil and bake in the oven for 45 minutes until the potatoes are tender.

Sprinkle with cheese and breadcrumbs and put under a medium grill until the top is browned. Garnish with parsley.

APRICOT AND ALMOND PUDDING

Serves 6

175 g (6 oz) unsalted butter

175 g (6 oz) caster sugar

2 eggs, beaten

25 g (1 oz) wholemeal self-raising flour

pinch of ground nutmeg

225 g (8 oz) fresh white breadcrumbs

175 g (6 oz) dried apricots, chopped

100 g (4 oz) blanched almonds, chopped

grated rind and juice of 1 lemon

2 tbls golden syrup

2 tsp milk

Cream the butter and sugar together until light and fluffy. Beat in the eggs. Fold in the flour, spice, breadcrumbs and remaining ingredients. Spoon into a 1.2 litre (2 pint) buttered basin or mould.

Cover with pleated, double-thickness, greased greaseproof paper and pleated foil. Put in a large saucepan of boiling water and steam for 2 hours, replenishing the water when necessary.

Serve with whipped cream, thick yoghurt, brandy sauce, or brandy butter.

This pudding will freeze for 6 months or can be stored in the refrigerator for one week. Steam for 45 minutes to reheat.

·CHILDREN'S CHRISTMAS·

If you are planning to have your Christmas dinner in the evening it may be more practicable to give the children a special Christmas feast of their own at lunchtime. The menu is planned for six children but could easily be doubled up for a bigger party. Older children and young teenagers will enjoy Crunchy Chicken and Peppermint Ice Cream Mice just as much as the smaller children!

To create a festive atmosphere it's fun to have individual place settings for each child. Start with brightly coloured paper plates and napkins, then add a jolly paper hat or maybe a balloon with the child's name drawn in felt pen, so that when it's blown up the name expands! There are endless ways to make the meal full of gaiety – just use your imagination and watch the children's faces light up!

CHRISTMAS CRACKERS

Serves 6

9 sheets filo pastry (strudel leaves) or 450 g (1 lb) puff pastry
75 g (3 oz) margarine or butter, melted
18 cocktail-sized frankfurters (or cooked sausages)
6 tbls smooth chutney
mint leaves, to garnish

Heat the oven to 220°C, 425°F, Gas Mark 7. Lay out the sheets of pastry on a work surface and keep them moist under a damp teatowel. Take one sheet of filo pastry at a time. Cut in half widthwise to give two small rectangles. Brush with melted margarine. Place a frankfurter at one short side and spread a teaspoon of chutney on it. Roll up the sausage inside the pastry, working from the short side. If you are using puff pastry, roll it out thinly, cut into rectangles and wrap once round the frankfurters.

Pinch the pastry at either side of the frankfurter to resemble a cracker and brush again with margarine. Repeat to use the remaining ingredients to make 18 crackers.

Place the crackers on a baking sheet and bake in the oven for 10 minutes until golden brown. Serve hot, with extra chutney if desired, and garnished with mint leaves.

CRUNCHY CHICKEN WITH TOMATO DIP

Serves 6

4 chicken breasts, skinned and boned
1 egg, beaten
4 packets unsalted crisps
¼ tsp dry mustard
¼ tsp paprika
salt and pepper
margarine or butter, for greasing
For the tomato dip:
50 g (2 oz) full fat soft cheese, softened
150 ml (¼ pint) natural yoghurt
2 tbls tomato relish
2 tbls finely diced green pepper
salt and pepper

Heat the oven to 180°C, 350°F, Gas Mark 4. Cut the chicken pieces into chunks about 2.5 × 1 cm (1 × ½ inch) and dip them in beaten egg to coat them thoroughly.

Pierce the crisp bags and crush the crisps in them, using a rolling pin. Pour the crushed crisps into a bowl and mix in the mustard, paprika and seasoning. Toss the coated chicken chunks in the mixture. Grease baking sheets with margarine or butter and place the chicken chunks on the sheets. Bake in the oven for 15–20 minutes or until the chicken is tender.

For the tomato dip, blend the cheese gradually into the yoghurt until the mixture is smooth. Stir in the tomato relish and the green pepper and season to taste.

Serve the hot chicken chunks on cocktail sticks ready to dip, accompanied by sticks of raw carrot, red pepper, green pepper and celery.

Variation: Instead of using chicken pieces, you can also use drumsticks for the children to eat with their fingers. Increase the baking time to 30–40 minutes and serve the dip on the individual plates.

MENU

Crunchy chicken with tomato dip
Crudités

•

Christmas 'crackers'

•

Peppermint ice mice
Cold Christmas pudding

•

Christmas sunrise

PEPPERMINT ICE MICE

Serves 6

300 ml (½ pint) milk

2 egg yolks

50 g (2 oz) caster sugar

2 tsps cornflour

300 ml (½ pint) double cream, whipped

½ tsp peppermint essence, or to taste

few drops green colouring

To decorate:

liquorice strips

flaked almonds

silver dragees

Whisk the egg yolks and sugar together until very light and thick. Blend the cornflour with a little of the milk to a smooth cream. Strain the remaining milk on to the egg yolk mixture and whisk until blended. Stir in the cornflour.

Set the mixture in a bowl over a pan of simmering water. Cook until the mixture coats the back of a wooden spoon.

Cool the custard, pour into a shallow container and freeze until of a mushy consistency. Turn out and whisk until smooth. Fold in the cream, peppermint essence and a few drops of colouring. Pour into a container, cover, and freeze until solid.

Allow to soften in the refrigerator for 1 hour before serving. To serve, scoop out small and large rounds of ice cream for heads and bodies. Push in strips of liquorice for tails, flaked almonds for ears and two silver dragee eyes, to represent mice.

Clockwise from top: Christmas crackers; Crunchy chicken with tomato dip; Cold Christmas pudding; Christmas sunrise; Peppermint ice mice

COLD CHRISTMAS PUDDING

Serves 6

75 g (3 oz) white fondant icing or white marzipan
few drops of green food colouring
2 packets strawberry or raspberry jelly
75 g (3 oz) sultanas
50 g (2 oz) glacé cherries, halved
25 g (1 oz) blanched almonds, chopped
15 g (½ oz) angelica, chopped
a little whipped cream, to decorate

Make holly leaves by kneading the fondant with green food colouring. Roll out to 5 mm (¼ inch) thickness between sheets of greaseproof paper, dusting with icing sugar to prevent the mixture from sticking. Cut out the leaves with a cutter or cardboard template. Lay the leaves over the rolling pin to give them a slight curve and leave to dry overnight.

Make up the jelly according to pack directions, using 2 fl oz (50 ml) less water than directed. Leave the jelly to cool. When it is on the point of setting, stir in the sultanas, cherries, almonds and angelica. Pour the jelly into 6 small moulds and allow to set completely.

Turn out by dipping the mould in hot water for a few seconds. Decorate each pudding with a little whipped cream and the holly leaves.

Variation: Cold Christmas pudding can be adapted to an adult dish by making up the jelly with a mixture of water and sherry. A firmer jelly, which can be sliced with a knife and served with cream, is made by increasing the amount of dried fruit and nuts, perhaps also adding some pieces of preserved pineapple to the mixture.

CHRISTMAS SUNRISE

Serves 6

300 ml (½ pint) fresh orange juice
2 tbls lemon juice
600 ml (1 pint) lemonade, chilled
3 tbls grenadine syrup

Mix together the orange juice, lemon juice and lemonade and pour into tall glasses. Carefully pour the grenadine into each glass to that it sinks to the bottom, giving a sunrise effect. Serve with decorative straws.

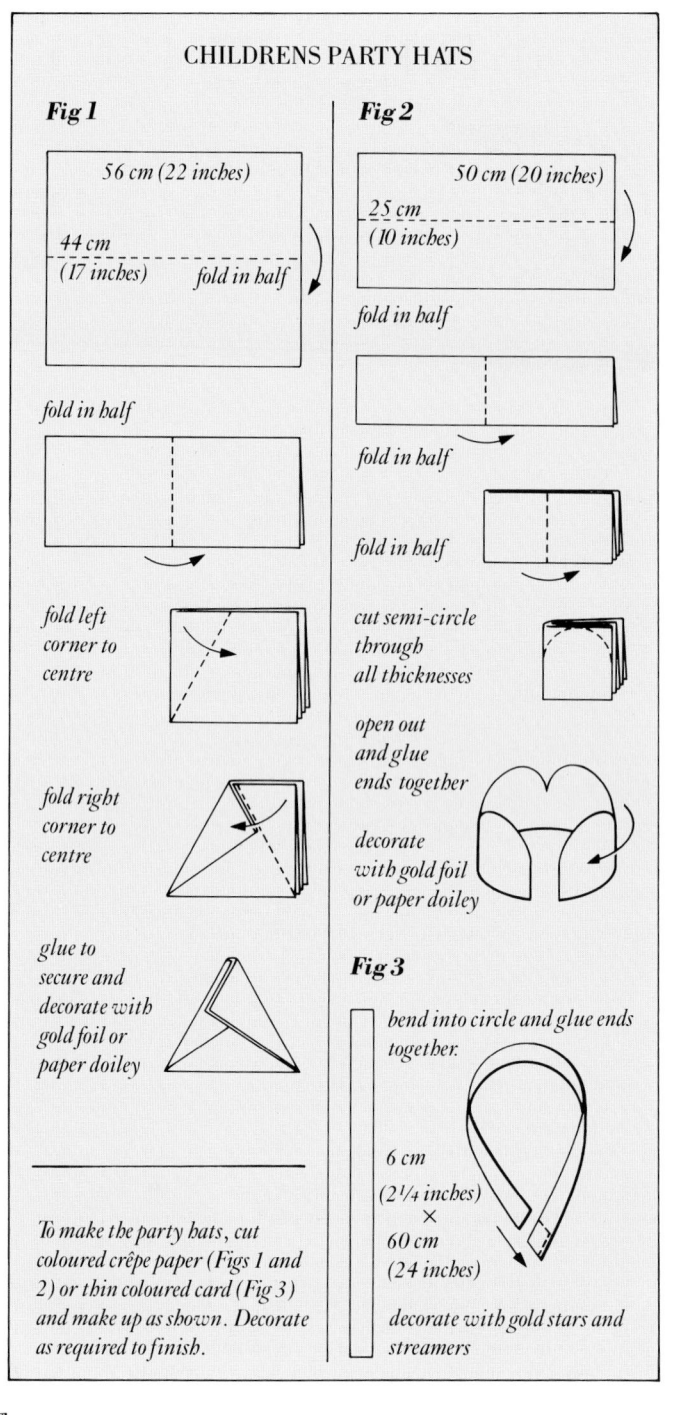

CHILDRENS PARTY HATS

Fig 1
56 cm (22 inches)
44 cm (17 inches)
fold in half
fold in half
fold left corner to centre
fold right corner to centre
glue to secure and decorate with gold foil or paper doiley

Fig 2
50 cm (20 inches)
25 cm (10 inches)
fold in half
fold in half
fold in half
fold in half
cut semi-circle through all thicknesses
open out and glue ends together
decorate with gold foil or paper doiley

Fig 3
bend into circle and glue ends together.
6 cm (2¼ inches) × 60 cm (24 inches)
decorate with gold stars and streamers

To make the party hats, cut coloured crêpe paper (Figs 1 and 2) or thin coloured card (Fig 3) and make up as shown. Decorate as required to finish.

· THE GINGERBREAD HOUSE ·

Fig 1

The story of Hansel and Gretel and the wondrous, eatable house in the woods still catches the imagination of children. The charming version pictured stands about 24 cm (9½ inches) high and would make a delightful centrepiece for a children's party table – or it could be placed on a side table as part of the Christmas decorations.

You will need:

675 g (1½ lbs) plain flour
3 tsps bicarbonate of soda
3 tsps ground ginger
225 g (8 oz) margarine
275 g (10 oz) dark brown soft sugar
8 tbls golden syrup
2 eggs, lightly beaten
For the royal icing:
½ egg white
225 g (8 oz) icing sugar, sifted
½ tsp lemon juice

Heat the oven to 190°C, 375°F, Gas Mark 5. Grease the baking sheets. Sift together flour, bicarbonate of soda and ground ginger. Rub in the fat until the mixture is the consistency of breadcrumbs, then add the sugar. Mix well.

Warm the syrup to make it flow easily and stir into the mixture with the eggs to make a pliable, soft dough. Knead until smooth.

Roll out to about 4 mm (¼ inch) thickness on greased baking sheets. Using the card templates, cut out the shapes (see diagram) and trim off the excess dough. Cut a diamond window out of the front gable and place a boiled sweet in the middle (during baking this will melt and form a stained glass window). Bake in the oven for about 10 minutes until evenly coloured. If any pieces have become misshapen during baking place the relative template on top of the piece and trim the edges while the biscuit is still warm. Allow the pieces to cool for up to 24 hours before starting the assembly.

To make the royal icing, whisk the egg white to a light froth and beat in the icing sugar a spoonful at a time. Beat in the lemon juice. Do not try to beat the mixture too stiffly – the icing should be of sufficiently soft consistency to hang from the eaves like melting snow.

Assemble on a 30 cm (12 inch) diameter cake board. Using a piping bag filled with royal icing, apply icing to the bottom edge and one side of the house. Quickly apply icing to the bottom edge of one end (gable) and position the side and end on the board. The icing will hold them in place.

Apply icing to the bottom edge and other side of the house and place in position. Fix the second gable in position in the same way.

Apply the eaves to the faces of the gables with icing. Assemble the roof panels after coating the top of the walls with icing.

Add the balcony, door and window shutters, using icing, and hold in place until the icing begins to harden.

It does not matter if there are gaps along the joins between the walls because you will be able to hide them with the decoration you add to the house.

To decorate

Gingerbread houses are traditionally decorated with sweets. Use any or all of the following: chocolate flakes, chocolate matchsticks, jelly diamond cake decorations for the roof tiles; barley sugar sticks for the balcony supports; chocolate covered finger biscuits for the roof ridge. 'Paddle' the soft icing to and fro so the eaves appear to be dripping with snow and icicles. Fix all decorations with royal icing.

Pipe royal icing around balcony edge and window shutters, catches etc. Inside the house, place a few coins of chocolate money, loose Smarties, humbugs and so on so that they can be seen through the doors and windows. Make a picket fence by painting lollipop sticks white and glueing them together.

Making templates

From the diagram Fig 1, draw the shapes on paper (the scale of the pattern is 1 square = 2.5 cm (1 inch). Using carbon paper, trace the shapes down onto stiff cardboard. Mark in all the annotation so that you can easily identify each template.

EAVES – cut 2

WINDOW SHUTTERS cut 8

SIDES – cut 2

BALCONY – cut 1

ROOF PANEL – cut 2

Fig 1 CONT.

FRONT GABLE
cut 1

fix balcony here *fix eaves 1 here*

DOOR – *cut 1*

BACK GABLE
cut 1

fix eaves 2 here

The Gingerbread house, shown here in a sugar 'snow' landscape.

· BOXING DAY ·

Boxing Day was traditionally a day when Christmas gifts – 'boxes' – were presented. In modern times it has become a day for lunchtime entertaining when friends call either for drinks and nibbles or for a light lunch. There will be comings and goings as people visit the family they have not managed to see on Christmas day itself, and children will be busy playing with new toys. All in all, Boxing Day tends to be a more rushed and busy day than Christmas Day itself, when the family group settles down together.

It is also a day when things can seem a little 'flat' after the excitement of Christmas, so keep the festive feeling by offering special delicacies to eat and drink. Display Christmas presents amongst the greenery on bookshelves and mantelpieces to give a new look to the Christmas decorations and have to hand some card or board games to keep the party spirit going.

Following so soon after the Christmas feast the dishes served for this post-celebration day need to be a little unusual to tempt possibly jaded palates. The Tandoori kebabs can be served as a starter or simply as an accompaniment to drinks. The Shellfish terrine and Turkey mango risotto are 'fork' meals, while the Coffee vanilla bavarois and the Pineapple kirsch crêpes make exotic and mouth-watering desserts.

PLANNING AHEAD

Tandoori pork kebabs Make these the day before and marinate them for 24 hours before cooking.

Shellfish terrine Make this 36 hours in advance and keep chilled, covered.

Turkey mango risotto Make and freeze 1 month ahead, without the mangoes. Reheat gently, add the mangoes and serve.

Radicchio salad Make fresh on the day, adding the dressing at the last moment.

Coffee vanilla bavarois Make 3 days in advance. Chill and keep covered.

Pineapple kirsch crêpes Make and freeze up to 3 months ahead. Thaw at room temperature the day before. Keep covered and chilled until needed. Make the sauce just before serving.

TANDOORI PORK KEBABS

Kebabs make an ideal dish for light entertaining, being easy and informal – but exotic enough for an occasion.

Serves 6
1 medium onion, chopped
2 garlic cloves, crushed
2 tbls grated ginger root
finely grated rind and juice of ½ lemon
250 ml (8 fl oz) natural yoghurt
1 tbls ground coriander
1 tsp each ground cumin, chilli powder, turmeric, garam marsala, mixed spice
freshly ground black pepper
4 tbls olive oil
750 g (1½ lb) pork fillet, cut into cubes
To garnish:
sliced onion
lemon wedges
coriander leaves

Place the onions, garlic, ginger, lemon rind and juice in a processor or liquidizer and blend to a smooth paste. Add the yoghurt, spices, pepper and oil. Mix thoroughly.

Place the pork cubes in the yoghurt mixture and turn them so that they are completely covered. Cover and leave to marinate in the refrigerator overnight. Thread the cubes on skewers. Grill under a moderately high heat for 15–20 minutes, turning frequently and brushing with the remaining marinade.

Variation: You can add a few drops of red or orange food colouring to the marinade for a traditional Indian appearance to the tandoori. If you prefer your marinade hotter or milder, slightly alter the amount of chilli powder.

Tandoori food should, strictly speaking, be cooked in a clay oven – but since this is not practicable, an ordinary grill will do just as well!

MENU

Tandoori pork kebabs
Shellfish terrine

Turkey mango risotto
Radicchio salad

Coffee vanilla bavarois
Coffee sauce
Pineapple kirsch crêpes

Clockwise from top:
Shellfish terrine; Turkey
mango risotto; Tandoori
pork kebabs; Radicchio
salad

BOXING DAY

SHELLFISH TERRINE
Serves 6
350 g (12 oz) haddock, whiting or sole fillets, skinned

150 ml (¼ pint) dry white wine

1 bouquet garni

few strips of pared lemon rind

225 g (8 oz) skimmed milk cheese

225 g (8 oz) curd or full fat soft cheese

2 tbls gelatine

3 egg whites

1 tbls lemon juice

3 tbls chopped fresh chives

freshly ground black pepper

225 g (8 oz) cooked shelled prawns, thawed if frozen, roughly chopped

2 tbls tomato purée

few drops Tabasco sauce

To garnish:
cucumber slices

whole prawns

dill sprigs

Place the fish fillets in a shallow pan with the wine, bouquet garni, lemon rind and just enough water to cover the fish. Poach, covered, over a gentle heat for 8–10 minutes until just tender.

Remove the fish with a slotted spoon, drain, flake and cool. Reserve the cooking liquor.

Soften the two cheeses and beat them together until they are smooth. Place 4 tbls hot fish liquor in a cup and sprinkle gelatine over it. Stir until the gelatine is dissolved. Allow to cool. Stir into the cheese mixture.

Whisk the egg whites until stiff and fold into the cheeses. Divide the mixture into halves. Into one half gently stir the cooked fish, lemon juice, chives and black pepper. Pour this mixture into a wetted 1 kg (2 lb) loaf tin and chill until set. Into the remaining cheese mixture stir the prawns, tomato purée and Tabasco sauce. Pour on to the fish mixture in the tin and chill until set. If you are not serving the terrine immediately on setting, cover and refrigerate.

To turn out the terrine, dip the loaf tin into a bowl of hot water for a few seconds. Turn out on to a dish. Serve the terrine in slices, garnished with cucumber slices, prawns and dill sprigs.

TURKEY MANGO RISOTTO
Serves 6
2 tbls vegetable oil

1 medium onion, thinly sliced

2 sticks celery, sliced

1 green pepper, cored, seeded and sliced

1 red pepper, cored, seeded and sliced

275 g (10 oz) long grain rice

6 cardomom pods

½ tsp powdered saffron

25 g (1 oz) sultanas

25 g (1 oz) pine nuts (optional)

½ tsp ground mixed spice

freshly ground black pepper

600 ml (1 pint) chicken or turkey stock

750 g (1½ lb) cooked turkey, skinned, boned and diced

grated rind and juice of 1 lemon

2 small ripe mangoes, stoned and sliced

Heat the oil in a large shallow frying pan. Add the onion, celery and peppers and fry for 2 minutes.

Add the rice and cardamoms, saffron, sultanas, pine nuts, if using, mixed spice and pepper. Pour in the stock and bring to the boil. Lower the heat and simmer gently for 35 minutes until the liquid has been absorbed.

Stir in the turkey, lemon rind and juice. Reheat and simmer for 2 minutes to heat the turkey through. Just before serving, gently stir in the mango.

RADICCHIO SALAD
Serves 6
1 head round leafed lettuce

1 medium head radicchio

100 g (4 oz) green grapes, halved and pipped

For the dressing:
3 tbls vegetable oil

1 tbls wine vinegar or lemon juice

1 tsp whole grain mustard

Wash, rinse and dry the lettuce and radicchio leaves. Place in a bowl and add the grapes. Make the dressing by shaking all the ingredients together in a screwtop bottle or jar. Pour over the salad, toss gently.

COFFEE VANILLA BAVAROIS

Serves 6

4 egg yolks
75 g (3 oz) icing sugar, sifted
300 ml (½ pint) milk, scalded
1 tsp vanilla essence
15 g (½ oz) gelatine
2 tbls water
300 ml (½ pint) whipping cream, whipped
2 tbls coffee essence
1 - 2 tbls coffee liqueur

COFFEE SAUCE

Make a coffee sauce by stirring 2 tbls coffee essence into 150 ml (¼ pint) single cream. Serve with Coffee vanilla bavarois and with other coffee-based desserts.

Place the egg yolks and the sugar into a large bowl and whisk together until they are light and creamy. Whisk in the milk gradually.

Add the vanilla essence and set the bowl over a pan of simmering water. Cook until the custard has thickened.

Sprinkle the gelatine over the water in a small bowl over a pan of hot water and stir until dissolved. Add to the custard and allow the mixture to cool. Just before the custard begins to set, fold in the cream. Set aside one-third of the custard cream but do not allow it to set. Stir the coffee essence and liqueur into the remaining custard cream. Spoon the mixture into 6 lightly oiled moulds.

Place the reserved custard cream in a piping bag fitted with a large star tube and pipe into the centre of the coffee cream in the moulds while the coffee cream is still soft. Chill the moulds until set. Turn out by dipping the moulds in hot water for a few seconds and serve with coffee sauce.

PINEAPPLE KIRSCH CRÊPES

Serves 6

For the batter:

300 ml (½ pint) milk
1 egg
100 g (4 oz) plain flour
25 g (1 oz) butter, melted

For the filling:

1 small pineapple, cored and chopped
1 tsp ground cinnamon
1 tbls soft brown sugar
3 tbls sultanas
40 g (1½ oz) unsalted butter

75 g (3 oz) caster sugar
150 ml (¼ pint) unsweetened pineapple juice
rind and juice of 1 orange
3 tbls kirsch
fresh pineapple, to decorate

Top: Coffee vanilla Bavarois with coffee sauce; Bottom: Pineapple kirsch crêpes

Place all the batter ingredients in a food processor or liquidizer and blend until smooth. Pour a spoonful of batter into a pre-heated, greased pan and quickly swirl it around to cover the base thinly. Cook for 1−2 minutes, then turn over and cook the other side until golden (about 30 seconds).

Repeat with the remaining batter to make about 12 crêpes.

Mix the pineapple, cinnamon, brown sugar and sultanas. Divide between the pancakes and fold into quarters.

In a large shallow pan, melt the butter and caster sugar together until golden brown. Remove from the heat and stir in the pineapple juice and orange rind and juice. Cook gently until a smooth sauce develops. Warm the kirsch, add to the sauce and set alight. When the flames die down, carefully add the pancakes to the sauce. Reheat gently to warm through. Serve decorated with pieces of pineapple.

·NEW YEAR'S EVE·

The New Year is a time for reviewing the past year and for making fresh beginnings and New Year resolutions – and how better to do that than in the company of close friends, with good food and a celebratory drink or two?

It is a very special time, of course, in Scotland, where Hogmanay is accompanied by the observance of old traditions. The first person through the door at midnight should be a dark-haired man carrying coal – this signifies prosperity to come. The church bells peal out a special New Year chime, and, in the past, all the front doors were left open for people to wander in to join the celebrations. Tradition also says that the house must be sparklingly clean and that all bills must be paid! Traditional offerings to eat are shortbread and black bun – fruit cake encased in pastry.

It is a time for easy, rather than formal, entertaining, when guests like to mingle and swap stories, so a buffet supper is ideal for this occasion. Have snacks on hand throughout the evening for unexpected visitors, and invite your special guests for 9.30 with the buffet served at 10.30, taking the festivities through to the celebratory whisky or champagne at midnight. Make sure there are plenty of non-alcoholic drinks on hand, too, for drivers – and for those children who are old enough to stay up, who will very much enjoy seeing in the New Year with the grown-ups.

MENU

Buffet for 8–10
Roast chicken galantine

•

Spiced roast gammon
Bean and mushroom salad
Avocado and orange salad

Kiwi fruit ice cream
Linzertorte with raspberry cream

PLANNING AHEAD

Roast chicken galantine Can be cooked 1 month ahead and frozen whole. Thaw overnight, slice and serve.

Spiced roast gammon Cook and freeze up to 1 month ahead. Thaw at room temperature overnight, slice and serve.

Bean and mushroom salad Prepare fresh.

Avocado and orange salad Prepare fresh.

Kiwi fruit ice cream Prepare and freeze up to 1 month ahead.

Linzertorte with raspberry cream Make and freeze up to 2 months ahead.

ROAST CHICKEN GALANTINE

Serves 8–10
1.75 g (4 lb) chicken, boned
salt and pepper
225 g (8 oz) sausage meat
225 g (8 oz) minced veal
1 onion, finely chopped
1 tbls green peppercorns, drained
grated rind and juice of ½ lemon
2 tbls dry sherry
50 g (2 oz) pressed tongue, sliced
50 g (2 oz) mushrooms, finely chopped
4 tbls parsley, finely chopped
25 g (1 oz) fresh white breadcrumbs
1 tbls capers, drained and chopped
25 g (1 oz) butter, melted
1 tbls oil
parsley sprigs, to garnish

Heat the oven to 180°C, 350°F, Gas Mark 4. To bone the chicken, set it on a board breast side down. Make a cut through the skin along the centre from the neck to tail. Be careful not to cut the skin from now on. Scrape the flesh away from the bones, gradually working round the carcass, breaking the legs and wings away from the rib cage as you go. Cut off the end of the wing and leg joints, and pull out the rib cage. Using a small knife, scrape the flesh from the leg and wing bones. Remove the bones and save to make stock.

Spread the boned bird out on the work surface, skin side down. Fold the legs and wings towards the inside. Season the flesh. Trim the bird to a neat, rectangular shape. Spread a sheet of waxed paper or polythene over the flesh and beat with a rolling pin several times to even out the meat.

Mix together the sausage meat and the veal. Work in the onions, peppercorns, lemon rind and juice and sherry. Season with pepper.

Spread the mixture over the opened-out chicken. Lay the tongue over the filling. Mix together mushrooms, parsley, breadcrumbs and capers. Season, and lay it over the tongue.

*Left to right: Bean and
mushroom salad; Roast
chicken galantine;
Avocado and orange
salad; Spiced roast
gammon*

Bring up the sides of the meat to enclose the filling. Fasten with a skewer along the top. Bring up the ends and sew with a needle and cotton to make a neat, rectangular shape. Weigh the bird.

Place the bird on a large sheet of foil in a roasting tin. Brush all over with butter and oil. Close the foil over the bird. Bake in the oven for 30 minutes per 450 g (1 lb).

Open the foil, baste, and cook for a final 30 minutes until golden brown. To test if the galantine is cooked, insert a skewer and ensure that the juices run clear. Remove the bird from the foil and allow to stand on a rack to cool. Remove the sewing threads and garnish with parsley. Carve into slices to serve. The cooked bird may be frozen, whole, for up to one month.

SPICED ROAST GAMMON

Serves 8 – 10

2.25 kg (5 lb) ham, boned and rolled
1 bay leaf
½ small onion, peeled
1 carrot, cut into rounds
3 cloves
½ tsp black peppercorns
1½ tbls soft brown sugar
1½ tbls redcurrant or quince jelly
1 tbls whole grain mustard
½ tsp allspice
¼ tsp ground coriander
bay leaves, to garnish

Soak the ham overnight in cold water. (If this is not possible, place the ham in a large pan of cold water and bring to the boil. Remove the ham, discard the water.)

Place the ham in a saucepan of cold, fresh water. Add the bay leaf, onion, carrot, cloves and peppercorns. Bring to the boil, cover, and simmer for 1½ hours.

Heat the oven to 220°C, 425°F, Gas Mark 7. Remove the ham from the water. Peel off the skin with a sharp knife, leaving the white fat.

Place the ham in a roasting tin. Using a knife point, mark diagonal lines across the fat to make a diamond pattern.

Mix together the sugar, jelly, mustard and spices. Rub this mixture into the fat. Bake the joint in the oven for 30 minutes. Serve garnished with bay leaves.

BEAN AND MUSHROOM SALAD

Serves 8 – 10

439 g (15½ oz) can chick peas, drained
439 g (15½ oz) can red kidney beans, drained
439 g (15½ oz) can flageolet beans, drained
340 g (12 oz) can sweetcorn kernels, drained
100 g (4 oz) button mushrooms, sliced
1 bunch spring onions, finely chopped
For the dressing:
4 tbls salad or olive oil
1-2 tbls wine vinegar
salt and pepper
¼ tsp mustard powder
1 garlic clove, finely chopped

Mix together the peas, beans, sweetcorn, mushrooms and spring onions in a bowl, reserving a spoonful of onions for garnish. Put the dressing ingredients in a screw-top jar and shake vigorously. Pour over the salad and toss well. Sprinkle the remaining spring onions over the top.

Variation: You can alter this salad as you wish, using canned or seasonal salad vegetables. Try:

Bean and onion salad If red onions are available, use one instead of spring onions and omit the red kidney beans.

Four bean salad Substitute black beans and rose cocoa beans for the chick peas and sweetcorn kernels.

French bean salad Steam 225 g (8 oz) French beans for 15 minutes or until tender. Allow them to cool and add them to the salad in place of the sweetcorn kernels.

Rice and bean salad Omit the chick peas and flageolet beans and add 1 kg (2 lb) cooked long grain rice.

KIWI FRUIT ICE CREAM

Serves 8 – 10

600 ml (1 pint) milk
1 vanilla pod
4 egg yolks
175 g (6 oz) caster sugar
2 tbls cornflour
600 ml (1 pint) double cream, whipped
4 ripe kiwi fruit, peeled and cored
2 tsps lemon juice
100 g (4 oz) icing sugar, sifted

AVOCADO AND ORANGE SALAD

Serves 8 – 10

1 Batavia or crisp lettuce
1 bunch watercress
2 avocados, sliced
2 oranges, peeled, pith removed, and segmented

Mix all the ingredients together in a salad bowl. If you like, you can mix the orange juice with a little oil for a dressing.

Place the milk and vanilla pod in a large pan. Bring to the boil briefly, then remove from the heat. Allow to stand for 30 minutes.

Whisk the egg yolks and caster sugar until very light and thick. Blend the cornflour with a little of the milk to make a smooth cream. Strain the remaining milk on to the egg mixture and whisk until blended. Stir in the cornflour.

Set the custard mixture in one or more large, shallow bowls over large pans of simmering water and cook, stirring, until the mixture thickens enough to coat the back of a wooden spoon.

Cool the custard completely and pour it into a shallow freezing container. Freeze for about 3 hours.

Turn into a large bowl and beat until smooth. Fold in the whipped cream and return to the freezer until mushy.

Purée the kiwi fruit in a food processor or blender, reserving one for garnish. Stir in the lemon juice and icing sugar. Beat the semi-frozen ice cream until smooth again, then layer it back into the freezer container in large spoonfuls, alternating with the kiwi fruit purée. Freeze until solid. Soften for 1 hour in the refrigerator before serving, garnished with the remaining kiwi fruit, cut into slices. Serve with wafer biscuits (see Christmas Eve Feast, pages 14–15).

Variation: Try using mango instead of kiwi fruit for a different flavour.

LINZERTORTE WITH RASPBERRY CREAM

Serves 8 – 10
100 g (4 oz) plain flour
2 tsp cocoa powder
50 g (2 oz) caster sugar
¼ tsp ground cloves
½ tsp cinnamon
½ tsp baking powder
pinch of salt
100 g (4 oz) ground almonds
100 g (4 oz) butter or margarine
a little milk or kirsch
350 g (12 oz) raspberry jam
beaten egg, to glaze
For the raspberry cream:
150 ml (¼ pint) double cream, whipped
100 g (4 oz) frozen raspberries, thawed and puréed
1 tbls icing sugar, sifted

Sift the flour, cocoa, sugar, cloves, cinnamon, baking powder and salt together in a mixing bowl. Add the ground almonds. Cut the butter into small pieces and rub into the mixture. Mix lightly to a dry dough, adding a little milk or kirsch if necessary. Wrap the dough in foil and chill for at least 30 minutes.

Roll out two-thirds of the dough and lay it in a greased 18 cm (7 inch) loose-based tin. Spread the jam on top. Roll out the remaining dough and cut into 1 cm (½ inch) wide strips. Lay the strips in a lattice pattern over the jam. Chill the tart for 30 minutes.

Heat the oven to 190°C, 375°F, Gas Mark 5. Brush the tart with beaten egg and bake in the oven for 20–25 minutes. Allow to cool in the tin.

For the raspberry cream, stir together the cream and the raspberry purée. Add the icing sugar and put into a bowl. Serve with the torte.

Variation: You can save some of the dough strips to make a pretty edging around the tart and drizzle some icing sugar over the top to create a seasonal snowy effect.

You may also like to omit the raspberry cream and serve the tart with plain whipped cream instead.

Linzertorte with raspberry cream; Kiwi fruit ice cream

THE CHRISTMAS BOOK
· LOVING AND GIVING ·
GIFTS FROM YOUR KITCHEN

Christmas gifts that you have made yourself will be the most appreciated and, if your talent lies in cooking, what better gifts than those from your kitchen? Practically everyone, young and old, can be given an edible gift and if you are imaginative about the container, this becomes a secondary present.

Some of the recipes in Festive Fare (pages 8–13) make ideal gifts – a jar of pâté or box of shortbreads, for instance. In this chapter, you'll find recipes for cordials and flavoured vinegars, easy-to-make sweets and candies and, for people living alone, miniature fruit cakes and puddings.

Miniature puddings

For people living alone, make miniature Christmas puddings in teacups or small basins. To improve the flavour, prick the bottom of the pudding and spoon over a tablespoon of brandy. Store, wrapped in greaseproof paper and foil.

To present, wrap the puddings in clear film, then tie them into a square of decorative transparent paper and fasten with a pretty ribbon. Present a small pot of Rum butter or Brandy butter with the pudding.

HERB JELLIES
Use basic apple jelly to make a herb-flavoured jelly to go with hot or cold meats.

1 kg (2 lb) cooking apples, cut into chunks, skin retained
1.2 litres (2 pints) cold water
3 tbls lemon juice
5 tbls fresh or 2 tbls dried herbs
500 g (1¼ lb) granulated sugar for each 600 ml (1 pint) of juice
green vegetable colouring (optional)

Put the apples in a pan with the water and lemon juice. Add the herbs in a muslin bag. Bring to boil and cook the apples until soft, mashing occasionally with a wooden spoon.

Remove the herbs. Put the pulp into a jellybag to drip overnight. Measure the juice and put it in a preserving pan with sugar. Heat gently, stirring, until the sugar is dissolved.

Test the taste and if necessary prepare another bag of herbs. Tie to a stick or a wooden spoon and support it over the preserving pan. Bring the jelly to the boil and boil until setting point. Remove herbs. Add colouring if desired. Pour the jelly into jars or glasses. Cover and seal.

SPICED NUTS

100 g (4 oz) caster sugar
1 tsp cinnamon
½ tsp ground ginger
pinch of ground nutmeg
½ tsp ground coriander
1 egg white
50 g (2 oz) each of shelled walnuts, blanched almonds, shelled hazelnuts

Heat the oven to 180°C, 350°F, Gas Mark 4. Mix the sugar and spices together in a bowl. Beat the egg white. Dip each nut in the egg white to coat it, then drop into the spice and sugar mixture, tossing until the nut is covered.

Place the nuts, spaced so that they do not touch, on a lightly oiled baking sheet. Bake in the oven for about 20 minutes.

Remove the tray of nuts from the oven, sprinkle with the remaining sugar and spice mixture and return to the oven for another 5 minutes. Allow the nuts to cool and then pack on layers of greaseproof paper.

TIPSY PRUNES

These improve with keeping so make them for gifts at least 3 or 4 months ahead.

Makes 2 × 450 g (1 lb) jars

600 ml (1 pint) cold tea
450 g (1 lb) demerara sugar
450 g (1 lb) prunes
300 ml (½ pint) port or sherry

Put the cold tea and sugar together in a pan and heat to boiling, stirring all the time. Simmer for 15 minutes. Add the prunes and cook them until tender (about 40 minutes).

Put the prunes into sterilized jars, using a slotted spoon. Pour in sufficient alcohol to come half-way up the jars. Fill with remaining syrup. Cover and seal the jars.

FLAVOURED VINEGARS

Flavoured vinegars are delicious for salad dressings and they are not difficult to make. Choose slim-necked white wine bottles for presenting.

HERB VINEGAR

Tie 1 cupful of herbs – tarragon, rosemary and thyme are good flavours – into a piece of muslin. Infuse in 1 litre (1¾ pints) of good quality wine vinegar for about a week. Remove the herbs and bottle the vinegar.

GARLIC VINEGAR

Mix 3 tsps of garlic purée with a little sea salt and blend in 600 ml (1 pint) of good quality wine vinegar. Bottle.

WAX TOPPING

Jellies and preserves for gifts can be packed into glasses, tumblers, large wine glasses, brandy snifters etc. and topped with a layer of paraffin wax. Buy this fresh from a chemist, melt it in a bowl over hot water and simply pour over the preserve. It seals the food and looks like a white 'head' on top of the glass. Cover with clear film and tie a bow of ribbon round the glass. Fresh paraffin wax is re-usable and does not affect the taste of food.

Clockwise from top: Tipsy prunes; Herb sachet; Herb jelly; Christmas ring; Caramel shortbreads; Cherry brandy jellies; Truffles; Fruit chews; Marzipan petit fours; Florentines; Spiced nuts; Miniature pudding; Herb vinegar

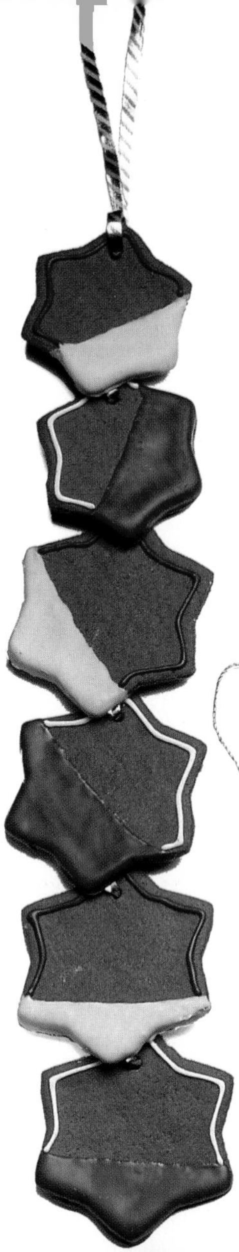

CHRISTMAS RING

225 g (8 oz) pack of puff pastry

For the filling:

100 g (4 oz) ground almonds

75 g (3 oz) caster sugar

finely grated rind of 1 lemon

salt

1 small egg beaten

To decorate:

apricot jam

glacé cherries, washed, dried and halved

candied peel

almond flakes, lightly toasted

Make the filling first. Mix the ground almonds, sugar and lemon rind with a pinch of salt. Bind with half the beaten egg to make a stiff mixture.

Knead on a surface dusted with icing sugar then roll into a 'rope' about 21 × 2.5 cm (9 × 1 inch) with the hands. Wrap in cling film and chill in the refrigerator for 1 hour.

Heat the oven to 220°C, 425°F, Gas Mark 7. Roll out the pastry to make an oblong shape about 33 × 13 cm (13 × 5 inches) wide and about 3 mm (⅛ inch) thick. Lay the rope of filling along the pastry, then bring the sides up and seal, moistening the edges with a little water.

Form the pastry into a ring, bringing the ends together and joining the pastry with a little water. Lay the ring on a floured baking sheet, join side down. Brush with the remaining beaten egg. Bake in the oven for about 30 minutes, until the top is golden brown.

While the Christmas Ring is still hot, brush warmed apricot jam over the surface and decorate with glacé cherries, pieces of candied peel and almond flakes.

Variation: The Christmas Ring can also be decorated with a little glacé icing drizzled over the top after the fruit and nuts have been added.

Biscuits and petit fours

Biscuits make a gift on their own, either packed into a brightly coloured card box lined with lace paper doyleys, or tied into bags of coloured clear film, with a large ribbon bow. The biscuits can also be rolled in film to make a tube with a strip of foil tied around the middle to simulate the cracker shape.

Biscuits can also be added to a hamper of bought foods gifts (pages 46 – 47) or can be an additional gift, perhaps packed into a flower pot with a few packets of seeds, or into a porcelain jelly mould with some boxes of spices and a wooden spoon.

CARAMEL SHORTBREADS

Makes about 16

150 g (5 oz) unsalted butter

100 g (4 oz) caster sugar

275 g (10 oz) plain flour

For the filling:

25 g (1 oz) butter

100 g (4 oz) caster sugar

2 tbls golden syrup

400 g (14 oz) can condensed milk

100 g (4 oz) plain chocolate, broken up

Heat the oven to 180°C, 350°F, Gas Mark 4. Grease a 30 × 23 cm (12 × 9 inch) Swiss roll tin. Cream the butter with the sugar, then gradually work in the flour. Press the mixture into the tin. Bake in the oven for 15 – 20 minutes until golden. Leave to cool. For the

MARZIPAN PETIT FOURS

Makes about 1 kg (2 lb)

2 × 225 g (8 oz) pkts golden marzipan

food colourings

angelica

cloves

glacé cherries

caster sugar

Divide the marzipan into small pieces and colour with the food colourings. Make fruits in proportion to each other – strawberries, cherries, apricots, plums, greengages – and form small bunches of grapes by pressing small balls of violet-tinted marzipan together with a little egg white. Cut strips of angelica for stalks and leaves, and press cloves into the ends of fruit for decoration.

Dust the finished fruits with caster sugar and leave to dry before storing in an airtight tin until needed.

Left: decorative Christmas ginger biscuits (recipe as Gingerbread house, page 32)

CLEOPATRA'S SWEETMEATS
Makes about 550 g (1¼ lb)

100 g (4 oz) no-soak apricots

50 g (2 oz) candied orange or lemon peel, chopped

75 g (3 oz) shelled walnuts, chopped

225 g (8 oz) seedless raisins, chopped, or whole sultanas

2 tbls orange juice

Process all the ingredients together. Roll into 2.5 cm (1 inch) balls and flatten slightly. Leave to dry then store in paper cases in an airtight jar or tin.
Variation: *Roll the balls in desiccated coconut or sesame seeds before flattening them. Chopped mixed fruit can be used in this recipe but home-made candied peel is better.*

---

filling, place the butter, sugar, syrup and condensed milk in a saucepan and heat gently until the sugar has dissolved, stirring occasionally.

Increase the heat and boil for 5 minutes, stirring continuously. Remove from the heat, leave to cook for 1 minute, then pour on to the shortbread base. Leave to set.

Place the chocolate in a small bowl over a pan of hot water and stir over gentle heat until melted. Spread over the filling.

Mark into squares and leave to cool completely before cutting into pieces and removing from the tin.

FLORENTINES
Makes about 12

50 g (2 oz) unsalted butter

50 g (2 oz) caster sugar, vanilla flavoured

1 tbls double cream, whipped

25 g (1 oz) chopped mixed peel

25 g (1 oz) glacé cherries, washed, dried and chopped

25 g (1 oz) angelica, chopped

15 g (½ oz) blanched flaked almonds

15 g (½ oz) plain flour

175 g (6 oz) plain chocolate, broken up

Heat the oven to 180°C, 350°F, Gas Mark 4. Melt the butter in a saucepan slowly. Stir in the sugar and the cream, and slowly bring to the boil. Boil for about 1 minute, then remove from the heat. Cool a little.

Stir in the fruit and nuts, then the flour. Drop teaspoons of the mixture on to greased baking sheets (about 7.5 cm (3 inches) apart, because Florentines spread in baking).

Bake in the oven for 10–12 minutes or until the biscuits look brown at the edges.

Remove from the oven, leave for a few seconds to 'set', then lift from the sheet with a broad palette knife. Cool on a wire rack. They may harden while you are trying to lift them from the baking sheet. If this happens, return the sheet to the oven for a few minutes and they will soften again.

Melt the chocolate pieces in a bowl over hot water and then spread the chocolate over the back of the Florentines. Mark lines with a fork to decorate.
Variation: Drizzle a little glacé icing over the surface of the Florentines. Plain caster sugar can be used but sugar in which a piece of vanilla pod has been stored makes a delicious flavour.

CHERRY BRANDY JELLIES
Makes about 450 g (1 lb)

4 tbls gelatine

150 ml (¼ pint) water

450 g (1 lb) granulated sugar

1½ tbls cherry brandy

red vegetable colouring

50 g (2 oz) caster sugar

Dissolve the gelatine in 4 tbls of the water. Heat the sugar and remaining water together, stirring continuously, until the sugar has dissolved. Bring to the boil. Add the gelatine mixture to the syrup. Stir in the cherry brandy and the colouring, to make a rich, red colour. Pour the jelly into a wetted tin and leave to set for a day.

To finish, turn out the jelly on to a sheet of greaseproof paper, sprinkled with caster sugar. Cut shapes with fancy pastry cutters and roll in the caster sugar to cover them. Place in paper cases.

TRUFFLES
Makes about 450 g (1 lb)

225 g (8 oz) cake crumbs

1 tbls cocoa powder

2 tbls apricot jam, sieved

1 tbls rum or brandy essence

75 g (3 oz) plain chocolate, melted

To decorate:

75 g (3 oz) chocolate, melted

chocolate vermicelli

glacé cherries

icing sugar

Mix all the ingredients together to make a soft dough. Use as desired to make different truffle shapes. Leave the truffles to dry and then place in paper petit four cases.
Vermicelli truffles Shape balls about the size of a walnut, coat lightly in melted chocolate an roll in vermicelli.
Truffle logs Shape small pieces into log shapes, dust with icing sugar and mark with a fork to make a log bark effect.
Cherry truffles Roll the dough to 6 mm (¼ inch) thick, cut into 2.5 cm (1 inch) circles and place a half cherry on top. Cover with melted chocolate.

FRUIT CHEWS
Makes about 450 g (1 lb)

50 g (2 oz) dried pears

50 g (2 oz) dried apricots

50 g (2 oz) seedless raisins or sultanas

25 g (1 oz) thick set honey

25 g (1 oz) hazelnuts, ground

15 g (½ oz) desiccated coconut

50 g (2 oz) chocolate vermicelli

Process all the ingredients except the honey together. Work in the honey. Divide the mixture into pieces and roll into log shapes about 2.5 cm (1 inch) long. Roll each log in a mixture of hazelnuts and coconut, or in chocolate vermicelli.

To serve, place each chew in a petit four paper case.

·BASKETS OF BOUNTY·

Delicious festive foods are, for most people, the best Christmas present to receive. Delicacies, or unusual foods that might not be eaten at other times of the year, are welcomed at Christmas and can add so much to the happiness and enjoyment of the holiday. Christmas is a time when, traditionally, feasting with family and friends is perhaps more important than at any other time of the year. It's the season for rich, warming foods, puddings and cakes, pies and pâtés, rich sauces and desserts. Gifts of food, chosen carefully, can provide the extra items for Christmas that everyone can appreciate, and put the finishing touch to any entertaining they might be planning.

The recipes on pages 42 – 44 provide some ideas for foods that can be cooked for gifts. The traditional Christmas hamper, bursting with festive foods, is an alternative way of presenting a gift of food, and there is no reason why a 'hamper' should not include both purchased foods and some delicacies cooked in your own kitchen. The wide range of foods available in modern supermarkets makes the planning of Christmas hampers comparatively simple and the expenditure can be spread over the weeks up to Christmas, choosing items along with your own pre-Christmas shopping. The baskets here have been planned for different life styles, from young people living alone to older, retired people, and will provide some ideas for the contents of your own hampers.

A Christmas hamper can contain several kinds of food, or just one or two, depending on the amount of money you want to spend. If just one or two items is the aim, choose related foods, such as a special cheese packed with a box of oatcakes, or cheese with a bottle of port. Christmas cake and a bottle of sherry make a good combination, and so do fine quality biscuits and a caddy of special tea. Pretty – or useful – baskets make good hampers and there are different kinds available. Small

round or oval baskets can be purchased quite cheaply and these are ideal for gifts such as a selection of cheese, or one or two small packets of foods. Larger baskets, intended as fruit baskets, can sometimes be found in crafts shops, and of course, there are bread baskets and shopping baskets in household departments and shops. Plastic storage baskets, which can sometimes be purchased from office suppliers, look surprisingly attractive dressed with bright ribbons.

Pack the gift foods in white or coloured tissue paper, arranging the paper as a kind of 'nest' for the boxes, jars and bottles.

A Christmas hamper wrapped to perfection, an inviting gift under any Christmas tree

FOR A FRIEND WHO IS A COOKERY ENTHUSIAST

Assorted, unusual herbs or spices
Cider apple herb stuffing
Cook bags
Garlic wine vinegar
Herb butter
Whole grain mustard
Peach chutney
Bottle of port

FOR AN OLDER PERSON LIVING ALONE

Shortbread fingers
Small madeira or fruit cake
Gingerbread
Comb honey
Scotch salmon bisque
Potted beef or salmon
Oatcake biscuits
Boxed cheese with herbs
½ bottle of red wine

FOR A GOURMET FRIEND

Ginger marmalade

Tuiles amandes

Smoked oysters or Lumpfish roe

Stuffed vine leaves

Lemon vinegar

Dijon mustard

Special Oatcake biscuits or Bath Olivers

FOR AN AVERAGE FAMILY, WITH LIMITED BUDGET

Chicken breast in jelly

Party sausages

Black cherry conserve

Crab pâté
or Chicken and herb pâté

Pickled walnuts

Bag of coffee beans or tea caddy box

Assortment of children's sweets

Christmas cake in a box or tin

Bottle of claret

RETIRED PERSON OR COUPLE

Cream of asparagus soup

Chicken breast in jelly

White wine cook-in-sauce

Packet of speciality tea

Redcurrant jelly

Dundee orange marmalade or honey

Assorted chocolate biscuits

Oatcakes

Piece of special cheese, such as Stilton

FOR A MAN

Lumpfish roe or Smoked oysters

Turkey pâté

Smoked salmon

Oatcakes

Acacia honey

Brandy snaps

Irish coffee chocolate

Bottle of white Burgundy

FOR A SINGLE PERSON

Cream of pheasant soup

Cured turkey breast

Asparagus spears

Apricot or peach chutney

Black cherries

Christmas pudding

Cumberland rum butter

1 cup coffee filters

Cognac truffle chocolates

Taco chips

Bottle of sparkling dry white wine

FOR A SMALL BASKET

Fruit cake

Coffee beans

Lemon marmalade

Shortbread biscuits

A Christmas basket overflowing with good things

THE CHRISTMAS BOOK
· DECKING THE HOUSE ·

Greenery — holly and ivy, laurel and fir — has been a traditional decoration for the festive season for thousands of years. In the dead of winter it brings the fragrance of the forests and the sense of being in touch with nature that we can all enjoy, no matter how urban our surroundings. Even with a minimal amount of arrangement, it gives an unmistakeable atmosphere of wassail and carols, feasts, good cheer and gift-wrapped surprises!

If you have holly in your garden the children will enjoy helping to gather it. Supply them with big baskets to carry it in and thick gloves to guard against the sharp prickles.

Greenery is also a symbol of success and eternal life, so make a door ring, hang some garlands, and dress the tree for a happy and prosperous New Year!

The Christmas tree

There is nothing quite like a real, fragrant Christmas tree, even though it sheds its needles for days, and, as trees rarely have a root when you buy them, it will die and be difficult to dispose of. Artificial trees of different kinds are available, but for an unusual look, cut a branch from a deciduous tree, paint it white and then touch the branches with silver paint or glitter dust. Suspend the branch before a mirror, or set it into a pot of plaster of Paris. Hang with silver and blue ornaments.

Mini trees are usually better for small rooms, or homes where there are no young children. Cones of florist's dry material oasis make good Christmas trees and are available in several sizes from about 15 cm (6 inches) tall to a sizeable 40 cm (16 inches) tall. Push a wooden dowel rod into the base of the cone, then fix the rod into a plaster-filled flower pot. Alternatively, press the cone's base onto the mouth of a large wine glass. The glass base will support the tree and look shiny and festive. Dress cone trees in red, green and gold wired ribbon bows, wired and folded circles of tissue paper (cut circles about 5 cm (2 inches) in diameter), sprigs of holly and small Christmas balls, tubes of fringed and wired gold foil, or even tufts of inexpensive lace, with silver balls pushed into the cone between the lace tufts. Victorians made miniature trees of dried flowers and these make charming displays.

For an elegant mini-tree, cover the cone with gold foil, then push pieces of glittering junk jewellery into the foil — brooches, earrings, rings etc. Beads threaded onto wire stems can also be used for mini-tree dressing.

A pretty tree can be made with strips of inexpensive gathered lace. Cover the cone base with foil, cellophane, or a scrap of plain fabric. Cut strips of lace to fit round the tree, and fix to the cone with glass-headed dressmaker's pins, to look like Christmas balls. Overlap the rows of lace up the tree, and finish with a large pearl or glass bead at the top.

Festive outlook

Dressing the house windows is a Scandinavian tradition. 'Snowflakes', made of crocheted lace and mounted in wire rings, are popular and traditional. You can get the same effect with lace paper doyleys, glued to circles of acetate, or hang sugar-stiffened crocheted doyleys (as described on page 51, Sugar baskets). Paper figures representing the Nativity are fixed to the panes, or 'stained glass windows' which are fun for children to make. For these, cut a piece of black paper or card, just a little smaller than the window pane, and cut some odd-shaped holes at random in the card. Glue some scraps of different-coloured film behind the holes – toffee papers are ideal for this.

To make attractive Christmas mobiles, cut shapes – birds, angels, stars, bells, trees – from double-sided crafts foil. Hang the shapes from threads and fasten to the top edge of window panes with a knob of plasticine. The slightest current of air will set them turning and spinning. For a pretty decoration both day and night, cut 15 cm (6 inches) pieces of red, green, or patterned crafts ribbons. Cut a scoop at one end. Cut yellow flame shapes from ribbon. Fasten the 'candles' along the bottom edge of window panes, using double-sided tape. You will find that daylight makes the candles look transparent, while from outside, at night, the house-lights make the 'candles' appear to glow.

Door ring

Ready-made rings of florist's block can be purchased for making door rings. You can make your own using a metal coathanger, sphagnum moss, cling film and binding wire. To decorate the ring, you can use sprigs of holly, sprigs of fir, gold-painted fir cones and thistle heads, fresh ivy tendrils, dried flowers and leaves, glass balls, 1 cm (½ inch) and 7.5 cm (3 inch) width ribbons.

To make the ring: Bend the hanger into a ring. Cover the wire with damp sphagnum moss, winding wire over it to hold it in position. Cover the moss with cling film and wind wire round the film.

To decorate: Holly and fir sprigs should be stripped so that sprigs with four or five leaves have a stem of about 7.5 cm (3 inches). Fir cones and thistles should be given a wire stem and most dried flowers and leaves will also need a stem.

Pierce holes in the cling film with a knife and push the stem of the decoration into the moss. Arrange so that the visual weight of material is at the bottom of the ring and the arrangement flows from the centre top to centre bottom.

To finish: Cover the wire hook with ribbon. Tie Christmas baubles on narrow ribbon and fasten to the hook.

Wire a ribbon bow from 7.5 cm (3 inch) width red ribbon and wire to cover the hook.

Garlands of greenery

Garlands are an ancient form of decoration which came to Britain with the Romans. There are several ways of making them but the simplest – and least expensive – uses florist's binding wire.

Garlands can be decorated with twisted ribbons, Christmas baubles, gold-painted dried material or simply left green and fresh-smelling. They can be used for wall decoration, for twisting round balusters or for the fronts of buffet tables. You will need a quantity of fir sprays or other evergreen trees or shrubs and florist's binding wire on a spool.

To make: Each spray is wired, in turn, to the stems of the others. Hold the first spray with spray 2 about half-way down the stem. Wire the two together. Add the third spray, halfway down spray 2, and wire all the stems together. (If you like, you can also tape the stems together with binding tape but it is not essential.)

Continue adding sprays, to the left and right, widening the garland as you reach the middle, then tapering off again towards the end.

To finish: With doubled binding wire, twist a hanging loop at both ends of the garland.

Deck the mantelpiece with a garland of greenery, tied up with bright red ribbons, and a pretty arrangement of dried flowers and leaves

·TABLE DECORATIONS·

Christmas is the time to let your imagination run riot on table decorations. Put a little thought beforehand into the size of your table, the number of guests you are expecting, and the food you will be serving. You will not want to constantly be moving your decorations to find extra space for dishes, and nor will you want to run the risk of greenery getting into the food – so if space is limited, content yourself with making small, dainty, decorations. On the other hand, if you have plenty of table space then you can add your decorations with a freer hand, making your table a feature of the festive living room.

oasis and the can. Push a candle holder into each block of oasis and put a candle in each (Fig 2).

Brush silver paint on the apples, leaves etc. as desired.

Variation: You can make a three-tier epergne by using a larger cake board as a base and two smaller ones for the tiers. Support each tier by glueing food cans to the cake boards. Glue oasis on the cake boards round the can on each tier. Arrange decorative material to fall in a pretty arrangement from each tier. Arrange material in the top can, or, if you want to use a candle, choose a shorter, thicker one.

A yule log, for the more traditional Christmas

MAKING THE EPERGNE

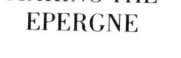
Fig 1

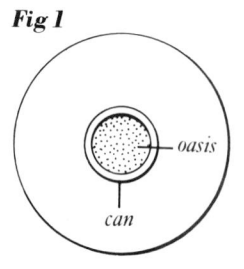
Fig 2

X = candle positions

SILVER AND GREEN 'EPERGNE'

For the epergne:
small can, label removed, washed and dried
dry material oasis
strong, quick-drying adhesive
20 cm (8 inch) silver cake board
To decorate:
paraffin wax, fresh small apples, wooden tooth picks, rose wire stems, ivy tendrils, Christmas roses, Christmas balls, tapers, candleholders

To wax the fruit, melt the paraffin wax in a bowl over hot water. Spear the apples on toothpicks. Dip into the wax once and leave to set.

To make the epergne, push the can into the oasis and it will press out the shape, filling the can. Glue the can to the centre of the cake board (Fig 1). Cut 4 × 2.5 × 7.5 cm (1 × 3 inch) pieces of oasis and glue to the cake board around the can.

Twist wire stems on the ivy, Christmas roses, Christmas balls etc. Push the stems into the oasis, arranging the material so that it falls over the edge of the cake board, concealing the

YULE LOG

You will need:
dry piece of driftwood or fallen wood or half a fire log, or a piece of petrified wood from a tropical fish supplier
plasticine or non-bake clay
To decorate:
candles, sprigs of holly or fir, fir cones, dried thistle heads small Christmas balls, ribbon bows etc., twisted onto wire stems

Find the steady side of the wood piece, and press plasticine or clay to the base to level it if necessary. Put plasticine or clay into any crevices and press the candles into the plasticine until secure. Arrange green and dried material around the candles to disguise the plasticine (see picture). Push wired cones, thistles, balls and bows between the sprigs of greenery.

You can make Yule logs large- or small-scale, according to the size of the log you begin with. Obviously, you will want to use different-sized candles in proportion to the design, from small tapers to large candles. White or red ones give the most seasonal effect. Simply add more or less greenery and fir cones to achieve the right balance.

MAKING THE SUGAR BASKET

Fig 3 — *mould*

pin edges evenly onto board until dry

CANDLE RINGS

Make Norwegian candle rings to set around thick candles, to set on shelves or side tables. These traditional rings can be found all over Scandinavia.

You will need:

sprigs of holly or fir
florist's binding wire
small glitter balls
wired ribbon bows or preserved flowers

Follow the technique for making garlands (page 49). Wire sprigs of greenery to each other, adding wired balls, ribbon bows etc. at intervals. Continue until the piece measures about 20 cm (8 inches) long, (or as long as required). Bring the ends together, to make a ring. Use glitter balls in colours to complement the colour of the candles — gold balls with red candles look truly seasonal. (In the summer you can make these exclusively of dried flowers instead.)

A delicate sugar basket to hold an assortment of waxed fruit

SUGAR BASKETS

Glistening sugar baskets are very easy to make and they are a good way of using old cotton crocheted mats which might have been put away and forgotten. They make effective and pretty containers for Christmas goodies.

Fill the baskets with sweets, dried fruit, nuts or Christmas balls for table decoration. If the mat is not too valuable, crocheted cotton can also be gold-sprayed. Thread gold or silver ribbons through the holes, or make handles by sugaring strips of insertion lace or bending florist's wire. The baskets can subsequently be washed to remove the syrup after Christmas is over.

Sugar baskets can also be used to present gifts of food or arrangements of dried flowers and leaves.

You will need:

50 g (2 oz) caster sugar for each mat
1 tbls water
a mould (bowls, glasses, dishes, etc.)
spray varnish (optional)
gold spray paint (optional)
florist's wire
satin ribbon

Stir the sugar into the water until it has dissolved, then bring gently to the boil. Remove the pan from the heat as soon as the syrup has formed.

Dip the crocheted mat or doyley into the syrup and squeeze out the excess sugar with your fingers.

Put the mould on a pastry board and place the mat over. Smooth it down the sides of the mould and spread out the decorative edges. Pin the edges to the board (Fig 3). The mats will take between 2 and 3 hours to dry out. After about 1 hour, the decorative edges can be bent to a particular pattern or shape if desired.

Remove the sugar basket from the mould and leave over-night in a warm place to dry out completely.

If desired, sugar baskets can be given a protective coating of spray varnish and the edges can be highlit with a touch of gold or silver paint.

Make handles by bending florists' wire to shape and wrapping with ribbon. Loop the wire handle through the holes in the rim of the basket and glue to the basket edges.

· NATIVITY SCENE ·

Fig 1a

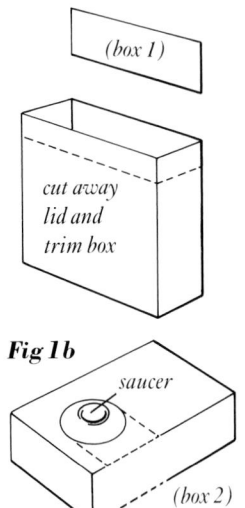

(box 1)

cut away
lid and
trim box

This charming Nativity depicts the birth of Jesus in Bethlehem, a Middle Eastern town complete with a palm tree in the inn's courtyard and the pale blue winter moonlight outside the stable. Empty food boxes are used for the stable and for the figures, with pieces of felt, beads, buttons, etc. to dress them. Smaller children could make a whole flock of salt dough sheep (the recipe is on pages 56–57), while older children construct the stable and make the figures.

Fig 1b

saucer

(box 2)

cut archways

For the stable:
2 × 250 g (8 oz) cornflake boxes
clear adhesive tape
instant adhesive
30 m (12 inch) piece of blue transparent cellophane
1 roll of white kitchen paper
white powder paint
30 × 45 cm (12 × 18 inch) base card
1 sheet grey or brown gift wrap
matchsticks
brown wrapping paper
13 × 13 cm (5 × 5 inch) piece of gold paper
1 sheet red patterned gift wrap
1 packet pink crêpe paper
thin white card
silver glitter dust
felt tip pens
7.5 × 25 cm (3 × 10 inch) piece of dark green felt
small food packet (e.g. stock cubes)
raffia
30 cm (12 inch) square of fawn felt
wood shavings or sawdust

For the figures:
thin white card from food boxes
2.5 cm (1 inch) diameter wooden or paper beads
coloured and white paper napkins
small elastic bands
20 cm (8 inch) squares of felt: light green,

dark green, black, bright blue, orange, grey-green
small pieces of coloured foil, or scraps of Christmas gift paper
beads, sequins and fringing for decoration
buttons and beads for kings' crowns and gifts
white tissue paper
13 cm (5 inch) piece of florists' wire

Accessories:
salt dough for sheep
brown wrapping paper and card for making donkey
small piece of parcel twine for donkey's tail

Fig 2

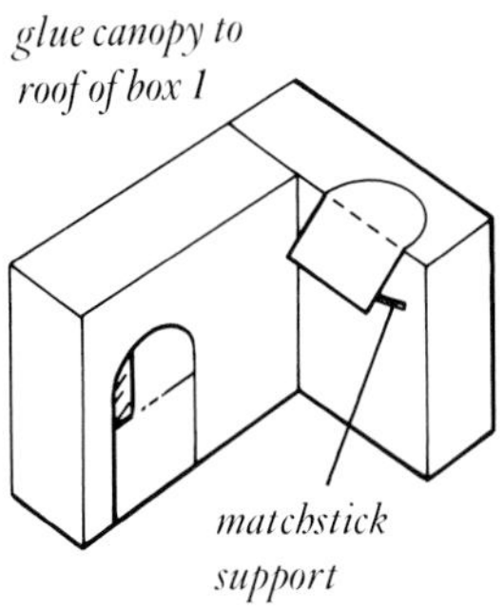

glue canopy to
roof of box 1

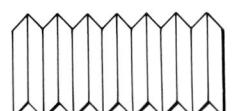

matchstick
support

1 Cut the lid from food box 1, then cut 2.5 cm (1 inch) off the top. Tape the lid back on and then tape closed (Fig 1a).

2 On food box 2, cut two archways (Fig 1b). Use a saucer to draw the curve. Glue the blue film behind the archway.

3 Glue or tape box 1 on to the end of box 2. Glue sheets of white kitchen paper over the 'walls' and roof of the stable. Glue the stable to the base card. Paint the 'walls' white.

4 To make the canopy, cover one of the cut-out arch shapes with grey or brown gift wrap. Fold it across the middle (Fig 2) and glue or tape the curved end to the roof of the box 1 stable section. Colour two matchsticks for supports and glue to the outer edge of the canopy and to the stable wall.

5 Cut a small door shape from brown paper and glue to the stable wall next to the archway. Cut a 10 cm (4 inch) diameter circle of gold paper and glue to the wall of the stable.

6 Cut a piece of pink crêpe paper 35 × 10 cm (14 × 4 inches) and fold under the edges. Glue to the roof of the stable section with the arch. Cut a second piece of pink crêpe paper 25 × 10 cm (10 × 4 inches), fold under the edges and glue to the other roof section.

7 Cut two strips 35 × 7.5 cm (14 × 3 inches) and 25 × 7.5 cm (10 × 3 inches) from the red patterned gift wrap and fold the strips along the length in concertina folds (Fig 3).

8 Glue the red paper 'tiles' to the roofs, firmly at the ends and lightly under the folds.

9 Cut a star from white card and glue it to a matchstick. Apply a little adhesive to the star and dust it with glitter. Pierce a hole in the stable roof and glue the star into the hole (see picture).

Fig 3

roof

Palm tree

10 Cut a 10 cm (4 inch) square of card, roll it up tightly and tape the join, to make the tree trunk. Glue coloured paper round it — or colour the trunk with felt tipped pens. Glue the trunk to a 5 cm (2 inch) square of card so that it stands up (Fig 4a).

11 Snip into the dark green felt all along one edge (Fig 4b). Wind the uncut edge of the felt round the top of the trunk, glueing as you go, and secure with an elastic band while it dries. Glue the palm tree beside the stable, pinning the base to the floor while it dries (see picture).

Crib

12 Cut the little food box down to 2.5 cm (1 inch) deep and cover the sides with matchsticks broken to fit the depth of the box. Fill the crib with shredded raffia, or alternatively you could shred the discarded pieces of box.

A charming nativity scene, fun for everyone to make. Shown here on a tray of sand, for maximum effect.

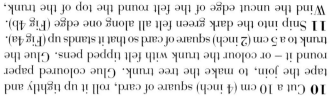

MAKING THE PALM TREE

Fig 4a
glue rolled trunk to square card base

Fig 4b
glue felt to trunk

secure felt to trunk with elastic band until dry

FIGURES

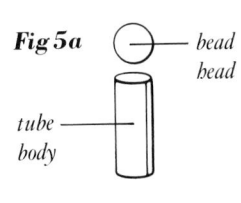

Fig 5a — bead head, tube body

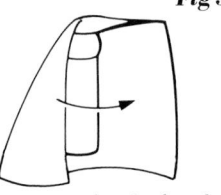

Fig 5b

secure edge of robe to head

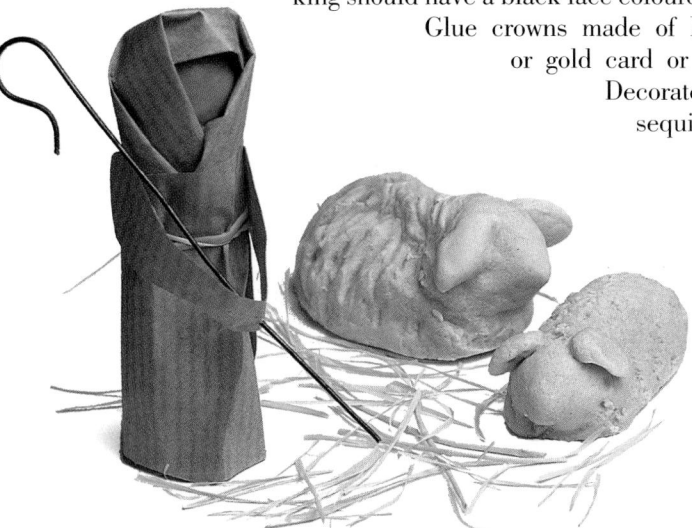

Fig 5c

wrap robe around body and secure with elastic band

A brown paper shepherd with salt dough sheep. A little shredded raffia makes excellent 'straw'.

Figures

13 All the figures are made on a cardboard tube base.

Cut pieces of card 6 cm (2½ inches) deep by 10 cm (4 inches) wide. Roll around a pencil to make a tube about 15 mm (⅝ inch) across. Glue a bead to the top of each tube, at a slight angle, so that the head appears to be looking downwards (Fig 5a).

Note: if you wish to make paper beads, soak small pieces of tissue in a water-soluble paste and roll beads, adding layers to make the bead larger. Leave to dry overnight.

Robes for figures

14 These are made from coloured paper napkins.

Fold one edge under and arrange over the bead head (Fig 5b). Fold the sides forward and across the 'chest' to the back. Secure with an elastic band (Fig 5c). Trim off level with the bottom of the tube so that the figure stands up.

Two of the shepherds are wearing white paper robes. The third wears a brown paper robe, but the technique for making it is the same. Joseph has a robe made of a yellow napkin.

Kings

15 Cut strips of foil or coloured paper to wrap around the tubes and glue or tape at the back.

Cut cloaks from felt (see Fig 6 for the shape) and secure around the Kings with an elastic band.

With a felt tip pen, draw hair on the kings' heads and one king should have a black face coloured in.

Glue crowns made of left-over pieces of red or gold card or buttons to the heads. Decorate their robes with beads, sequins or fringing.

Mary

16 Mary is made from a smaller tube, 5 cm (2 inches) high. Drape bright blue felt over the head bead, secure it with an elastic band, then turn the excess felt under the tube at the front. Trim to shape (see Fig 7).

Hands

17 All the adult figures have praying hands. Cut strips of card, (or fold crêpe paper or napkins), to 5 × 2.5 cm (2 × 1 inch). Fold once along the length and then once across the width (Fig 8a). Trim as shown by the dotted line (Fig 8b) and draw hands on the folded end.

Glue the open ends to the sides of the figures (Mary's arms tuck under her robes).

Glue the King's gifts (beads, buttons etc.) to the hands.

Bend the end of the florists' wire over into a crook shape and tuck it in the brown shepherd's arms.

Baby Jesus

18 Make a short, narrow tube body, and glue a smaller bead on for a head. Wrap the baby in white tissue, and glue in place. Put the baby in the crib.

The sheep

19 These are modelled from salt dough. Mark the fleece with a sharpened matchstick. Ordinary modelling clay can be used.

Donkey

20 Cut a piece of card 5 cm (2 inch) square and fold it in half. Wrap a piece of brown parcel paper around a small bead and secure with an elastic band. Wrap and glue more paper over and round the folded card, turning the edges under (Fig 9).

Cut two ears and glue to the head. Glue the head to the body. Colour a tiny piece of string with a felt tip pen and glue it at the back of the donkey for a tail.

Finishing

21 Cut a fringed end on the fawn felt for the stable floor.

Glue all the figures, animals and crib to the floor of the stable. Scatter wood shavings or sawdust lightly over the floor of the stable around the figures and animals.

Tie some raffia to resemble a bundle of straw and put it beside the stable.

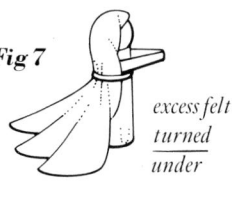

Fig 6 — cloak

MARY

Fig 7 — *excess felt turned under*

HANDS

Fig 8a — fold

Fig 8b — trim

DONKEY

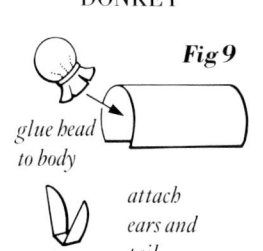

Fig 9 — glue head to body

attach ears and tail

body wrapped in brown paper

· CHRISTMAS TREE TRIMS ·

Many of the pretty Christmas tree trims in the picture on page 57 were made with materials you would normally throw away – food trays, egg boxes, cardboard food packets – plus a few inexpensive items for decoration.

Lace and roses These make very pretty tree decorations and the entire tree can be dressed with them. Use inexpensive nylon lace and gift ribbon or woven ribbon to make the flowers. Sew 1 metre (approximately 1 yard) of frilled lace into a circle (see picture). Sew ribbon roses to the middle of the lace circle. If you like, you can add fabric leaves. Add loops of narrow ribbon and a ribbon hanger.

This ornament can also be made with a paper lace doyley, by gluing the doyley to a circle of card, pleating the doyley as you work.

Stars Cut star shapes from white polystyrene food trays, dab with a little adhesive and press into glitter dust. Pierce a hole on one point and thread through white or gold string for a hanger.

Silver Bell Cut one section from a clear plastic egg box. Pierce a hole in the top. Cut a piece of silver kitchen foil and push it inside the bell, with about 6 mm (¼ inch) hanging over the edge. Cut the edge into points. Dab on a little adhesive and dip in green glitter dust. Push a shanked button inside the bell so that the shank protrudes from the top: the narrow ribbon through the shank for a hanger.

Gold bell Cut one section from a polystyrene egg box and cut another piece approximately 12 mm (½ inch) square. Cut a slit in the top of the bell, pierce a hole in the square piece and push the piece through the slit in the bell, hole end uppermost. Paint or spray gold. Dab adhesive on the mouth of the bell and dip in gold glitter dust. Thread gold twine through the hole at the top for a hanger.

Choirboys Cut circles of gift wrap foil, drawing round a cup or bowl to get the shape. Cut the circles in half, overlap the edges

---

and glue or staple to make a cone. Cut a circle from a white paper doyley. Dab a little adhesive over the foil cone. Draw eyes and mouth on the circle. Dab a little adhesive round the edge of the circle and dip into glitter dust. Tie a narrow ribbon or a piece of thread around the choirboy's neck. The arms are sections of white doyley glued at the sides and at the 'hands'.

Father Christmas Cut half-circles of coloured or white card. Cover the white card with gaily coloured paper or colour with felt-tipped pens or children's painting pens. Glue or staple into a cone. Glue on a blob of cotton wool for a beard and a bead for a nose. Thread a hanger through the point of the cone.

Teazles and cones Collect teazle heads and fir or pine tree cones and dry them. Paint gold and, before the paint has dried, sprinkle with glitter dust.

Pierce a hole in teazle stems for the thread hanger, wind the thread through the seeds of cones.

Silver star Collect some foil bottle tops and nightlight foil holders. Wash clean, press flat and cut into the edges. Lay the foil right side down on a soft surface (two or three layers of kitchen paper will do). With a toothpick or a blunt pencil draw a design in the centre of the star. On the right side, this will make a raised design. Decorate with beads or glitter dust.

This technique can also be used with heavyweight freezer foil but does not work with ordinary kitchen foil.

Lanterns These are best made either with double-sided gift wrap foil, or with freezer foil. Strips from colour pages from magazines also look effective but mount the pages on dark-coloured paper first. Cut a strip about 30 cm (12 inches) long by 7.5 cm (3 inches) deep. Fold lengthwise and snip into the folded edge. Open the paper out and overlap the short ends, staple or glue. Push the ends together to open the lantern. Make a hanger with foil or with thread or ribbon.

Lace and roses bouquet, ideal for hanging on the Christmas tree, or as a gift for a close friend. To make ribbon roses see page 58.

Round lanterns Make these either from foil or mount coloured magazine pages on a dark-coloured paper with spray-mount. Cut 4 × 20 cm (8 inch) strips of foil or paper, 12 mm (½ inch) wide. Join the ends of one to make a ring. Glue each strip in turn (Fig 1) until the four strips make a ball. Make a thread hanger.

Mini parcels For colour and glitter, wrap small food boxes in foil paper and tie with ribbons.

Ribbon balls Woven or gift ribbons can be used to decorate polystyrene or foam balls. Choose balls about 5 cm (2 inch) diameter. Cut ribbons and secure into the ball with dressmaker's pins (the kind that have coloured glass heads). The ribbons can be laid over each other or interwoven. Fasten a hanger with a pin. The coloured pin-heads become part of the decoration.

Salt dough decorations Cut shapes with cookie cutters or with a pointed knife. Bake (see recipe), colour with poster colours, felt tipped pens, coloured inks or with children's painting pens. Leave to dry, varnish if you like, decorate with beads or with glitter dust applied over a little glue. Remember to make holes in the ornaments before baking, so that a hanger can be threaded through.

Mini crackers Make these over long sweets, toffees etc. Roll the sweet in stiff paper (such as writing paper). Cut a piece of crêpe paper to go round the wrapped sweet and to about twice the length. Secure with a touch of glue. Fringe the ends of the crêpe paper (Fig 2), then wind a piece of strong thread round the cracker, just at the end of the stiff paper. Pull the thread ends away from each other to 'pinch' in the ends of the cracker. Decorate with scraps of foil or Christmas wrapping paper.

Christmas cookies Make a biscuit dough and roll out. When cutting out the shapes, push a matchstick through each cookie near to the top before baking, so that when the stick is removed, there is a hole for the hanger. Alternatively, tie a narrow ribbon round each cookie for a hanger.

Golden rings Use inexpensive plastic curtain rings of different sizes. Wind gold crochet thread closely round the rings (or use gift ribbons), finally knotting the ends together to make a hanger.

Ribbon balls in festive colours, for the more sophisticated Christmas tree

Shiny parcels Tie sweets or small gifts in coloured film and make a big ribbon bow.

Christmas trees You can make these of any shape – balls, diamonds, cones, etc. Use gift wrap foil or paper cut from magazine pages. Draw the shape on the foil or paper. Fold down the middle and cut out. Use this as a template to cut out two more shapes. Glue the three shapes together (Fig 3) to make the 'Christmas tree'.

Sunburst Cut the rims off two paper cups (white or coloured). Cut down to the bases in narrow strips and glue the two bases together. Glue sequins or coloured foil to the centres. If you like, spray silver or gold, or touch with glue and spray with glitter dust and decorate with coloured foil or ribbon. Attach gold twine to the outside centre as a hanger.

Velvet bells Push pipe cleaners or wires into velvet tubing (or satin, if you prefer). Twist into shapes – bells, trees, stars, fleur de lys – wire on some pretty beads for extra decoration and use gold twine as hangers.

Salt Dough Modelling

Salt dough is inexpensive to make, pleasant and easy to use and can be worked to make Christmas tree decorations that will last for many Christmasses to come. It's great fun for children to use and most of the ornaments pictured could be made by children between 8 and 12 years – but make sure they are aware that they are not edible.

SALT DOUGH
4 cups of plain flour
1 cup of table salt
1½ cups of cold water

Heat the oven to 150°C, 300°F, Gas Mark 2.

Mix the flour and salt. Add the water gradually to make a stiff dough. Knead thoroughly until a smooth, putty-like substance is achieved.

Working with Salt Dough

Salt dough dries out after an hour or two but you can make it flexible again by adding a little water on the finger tips and re-kneading. You can keep it in a plastic bag in the refrigerator overnight.

Roll salt dough with a floured rolling pin and cut out shapes

Fig 1

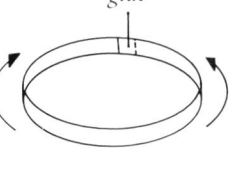
glue

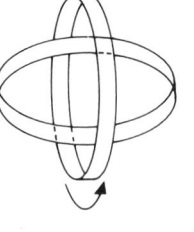

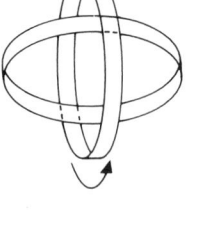

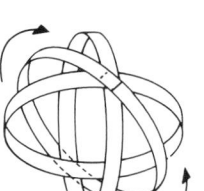

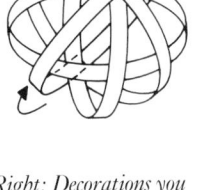

Right: Decorations you have made yourself add individuality and interest to the Christmas tree

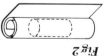
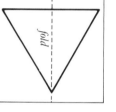

CHRISTMAS TREE TRIMS

using pastry or cookie cutters, a knife point or a knitting needle. Roll balls or thick rolls between the palms. Flatten shapes under the hand. Roll thin strips under a finger tip on a floured surface. Make discs by flattening small balls. Mark designs with kitchen tools, a knife point, graters, sieves etc. Join pieces by dampening the surface with cold water.

Work the shapes on a baking sheet or on a piece of kitchen foil so that they can be easily transferred to the oven. If you are planning to add beads, buttons and so on make an impression with them in the raw dough before baking and then glue the decoration into the baked indentation. Pierce holes for hangers before baking.

Leave shapes to dry out for about 15 minutes before putting into the oven.

Baking Ornaments

Salt dough takes about 2–3 hours to harden. If you want a shiny, brown finish, brush with a little condensed milk or a milk and sugar mixture. Thicker pieces, such as the sheep in the nativity scene, will take longer to bake and should be turned over half-way through baking.

Finishing

After the pieces have cooled they can be painted with poster paints and then varnished for a permanent finish. To create sparkle, dip the pieces in glitter dust while the varnish is still wet. Small shapes can be glued to larger shapes to create interest.

Father Christmas

Cut two round shapes with scalloped edges. Cut two crescents from one shape. After baking, paint one crescent white and the other red. Glue them to either side of the remaining round as a hood and beard. Stick on a sequin for the nose and bugle beads for the eyes. Glue cotton wool round the edge of the 'hood' and under the nose for a moustache.

Christmas pudding

Cut one round shape and two holly leaf shapes. After baking, paint a splash of white on one edge of the round shape. Paint the remaining area dark brown. Paint the leaves green and glue them on. Glue two red wooden beads on to the leaves. Stick sequins over the 'pudding' to resemble fruit.

MAKING THE MINI CRACKERS

Fig 2

roll sweet in crepe paper

pinch ends with strong thread

MAKING THE CHRISTMAS TREE

Fig 3

fold

cut out × 3 shapes using template

glue the 3 shapes together, inserting gold thread to hang

THE CHRISTMAS BOOK
· GIFTS TO MAKE ·

GIFTS TO MAKE

**MAKING
RIBBON ROSES**

Fig 1

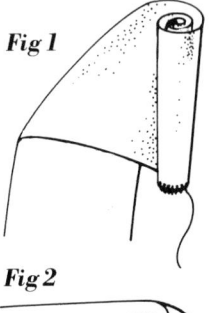

Fig 2

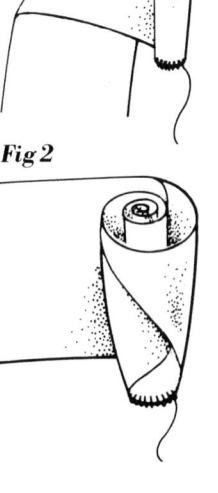

Pretty, romantic gifts, using lace, satin and silk fabrics, lustrous ribbons and fragrant pot pourri, have no price tag on them because they couldn't be bought in shops. Look for pieces of antique lace in specialist shops, or colour new cotton lace by dipping it in tea. The creamy look of dipped lace harmonises with pastel-coloured fabrics.

Lace sachets

Antique shops often have old lace mats or crocheted doyleys which can be used to make herb sachets with very little sewing. The rectangular sachet in the picture is made from an old wineglass mat.

Measure the mat and cut two pieces of thin fabric to the same shape and dimensions. Pin, baste and machine-stitch the pieces together, right sides facing, leaving one short end open for filling. Pour in the herbs and turn in the edges of the open seam, slip-stitching to close.

Sew the lace mat to the filled sachet. Make a ribbon rose for one corner and trim with 3 mm (⅛ inch) wide single faced satin ribbon. Thread a needle with matching thread and knot the end. Roll one end of the ribbon into a tight tube – about five turns. Oversew the end of the tube. Leave the needle and thread hanging. Hold the 'rose bud' in one hand and with the other, fold the ribbon end away from you making a diagonal fold (Fig 1). Turn the 'bud' onto the fold and keep turning the bud until the ribbon lies straight (Fig 2). Oversew the bottom end of the rose. Make another petal in the same way and oversew the bottom end. Make a third petal and sew. With the last 25 mm (1 inch), bring the ribbon end down to the bottom of the rose, gather and sew. Use the same thread to sew the rose in place. Tiny roses can be made with narrow ribbon for decorating sachets. The circular, pale green sachet is made from a small piece of embroidered organdie which has been edged with

25 mm (1 inch) wide insertion lace and then 25 mm (1 inch) wide lace edging. The filled sachet underneath is made from pale green moiré taffeta. Finish the sachet with a stitched bow of 3 mm (⅛ inch) wide green ribbon.

Herb sachets can also be made from pieces of ribbon weaving, but instead of hand-weaving and pinning ribbons, ribbons are woven with a darning needle.

Pin cushions

Use crocheted doyleys for making pin cushions, making them up in the same way as for sachets, but stuffing the 'pad' with polyester filling.

Pink pin cushion

Press a plastic bowl into a block of florist's dry material oasis so that the bowl is filled, then cut the block off level using a sharp knife. Cut a circle of bright fabric, 12 mm (½ inch) larger than the circumference of the bowl, place it on top of the filling and push down the inside of the bowl using a knife tip.

Cover with a scrape of lace or net, and push this down inside the bowl also. Glue a strip of gathered lace edging round the bowl, and then finish with a strip of lace insertion. Trim with a 20 cm (8 inch) wide ribbon sewn into a bow.

Patchwork pincushion

Using a 25 mm (1 inch) hexagon template (Fig 3), cut 14 fabric shapes and 14 backing papers.

Mount the fabric on a backing paper. Sew 6 hexagons round 1 hexagon, right sides facing, using small oversewing stitches. Make two 'rosettes' of patchwork in the same way. Remove the backing papers and place the two rosettes of patchwork together. Machine-stitch together, or hand-sew, using back stitches, all round the rosette shape, leaving sides of two adjoining patches open.

Turn the pincushion to the right side and fill with cotton wool

Clockwise from top:
Satin cushion; Covered
coathanger; Rose-
trimmed heart cushion;
Taffeta sachet;
Handkerchief sachet;
Patchwork pincushion;
Pink pin cushion;
Rectangular pot pourri
sachet

HEXAGON
TEMPLATE
Fig 3

repeat image
along dotted line

or polyester filling. Oversew the open seam. Sew on looped, narrow ribbons.

The same technique can be used to make a perfumed sachet.

Handkerchief sachet

The sachet in the picture is made with an antique silk embroidered handkerchief but new, lace-edged handkerchiefs could be used, or cut a 30 cm (12 inch) square of a delicate fabric and edge it with lace.

Cut a square of thin fabric in a pale cream (or white), 12 mm (½ inch) smaller than the handkerchief. Neaten the edges with machine-stitching, or hand-hemming.

Place the square on the wrong side of the handkerchief. Catch it to the handkerchief at the corners only. Fold three corners of the handkerchief to the middle (like an envelope) and catch them together with tiny stitches. Sew a ribbon bow to the outside of the sachet on the fourth corner.

If preferred, a sachet of fragrant herbs can be made from a scrap of organdie and slipped between the two layers of the sachet, so that handkerchiefs kept inside are perfumed.

Covered coathanger

PATTERN FOR
HEART CUSHION

Fig 4

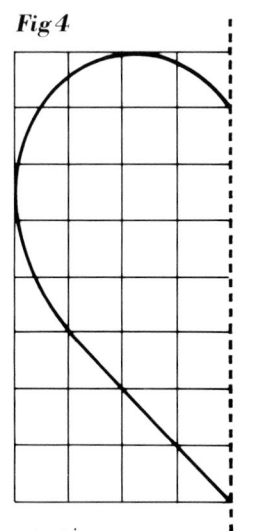

*repeat image
along dotted line*

Pad a wooden coathanger with strips of thin polyester wadding until the coathanger is rounded and the wood can no longer be felt through the wadding.

Measure the length and circumference of the padded coathanger. Cut a piece of polyester satin fabric to the measurements plus 25 mm (1 inch). Snip a hole in the middle of the satin and slip the cover over the hanger hook, right side out. Turning in the edges as you sew, slipstitch the cover round the coathanger, rounding off the seam at the lower edge and the ends. Cut a piece of wide lace insertion to three times the length of the hanger. Gather the lace 12 mm (½ inch) from one edge. Sew the lace along both sides of the hanger, along the bottom edge. Join the short ends of the lace with running stitches.

Thread a long, sharp needle with 1.5 mm (1/16 inch) wide ribbon. Take the needle through from one side of the hanger to the other, leaving a long end of ribbon. Bring the needle back through, 3 mm (1/8 inch) away. Knot the ribbon ends together or tie a small bow. Work knots at intervals along the hanger to produce a 'quilted' effect. Finish the hanger by winding 12 mm (½ inch) wide ribbon round the hook, sewing the ends together to secure. Tie a matching bow.

Rose-trimmed heart cushion

This pretty cushion, only 20 cm (8 inches) long, is filled with polyester padding, and a sachet of fragrant herbs is tucked inside, making it a charming bedroom accessory. Fig 4 is a pattern for a heart shape. To make a cushion of the same size, 1 square = 25 mm (1 inch).

Make a 20 cm (8 inch) deep sachet from sprigged fabric and, before making up into a cushion, cut lengths of narrow green ribbon and pin them across the sprigged heart shape, approximately 25 mm (1 inch) apart. Pin lengths of ribbon diagonally across to make a lattice pattern of ribbons (see picture). Catch the ribbons to the fabric at the intersections with cross stitches, using green embroidery cotton. Work a small pink French knot in the centre of each cross stitch. Ribbon roses are made with 9 mm (3/8 inch) wide satin ribbons, folded and stitched to make petals, working from the outside edge to the centre.

Finish the roses with yellow French knots for stamens. Work green satin-stitched leaves round the roses and finish the cushion front with 20 cm (8 inch) strands of embroidery cotton, threaded through the fabric so that 10 cm (4 inch) lengths hang. Tie a small bow of dark pink ribbon and sew over the strands of cotton.

Trim the cushion with ribbon bows and loops. Make up the cushion by machine-stitching back and front together, right sides facing, leaving a gap in the seam at the top of the heart for stuffing with cottonwool and a sachet of fragrant herbs. Push in the filling, arranging it so that the surface of the cushion is smooth. Close the seam with slip stitches, tucking in loops of the remaining pale green ribbon and the narrow pink ribbon. Sew guipure trimming round the heart.

Satin cushion

This is made with a bobbin lace tray cloth, dyed in tea to produce a soft, creamy colour.

To dye lace with tea, pour boiling water over 2 tea bags and then add 1 tablespoon of vinegar. Remove the teabags when the liquid is fairly dark. Steep the lace in the tea, squeezing it out periodically to check the colour. Rinse and dry. Spray-starch to stiffen the lace before mounting over a satin cushion. Thread narrow, cream-coloured ribbons through the lace, tying bows at the corners of the central panel. If preferred, a sachet of fragrant herbs could be tucked into the cushion before sewing the final seam closed.

PRETTY PRESENTATIONS.

Everyone loves to get a Christmas gift, no matter how small or simple it may be. If time has been spent wrapping it attractively, then the gift is all the more special.

Gift wrapping takes time and should not involve a last-minute panic and a dash around the shops looking for Christmas papers and red and green ribbons. Choose your wrappings earlier, in December, and make an occasion for all the family to enjoy, providing them with boxes collected in advance, a good adhesive, double-sided tape — and a pair of scissors for everyone involved. Here are 35 ideas for exciting gift-wraps.

1 Choose a theme for all the gifts — perhaps gold foil throughout — and use sections from white paper doyleys instead of ribbons.

2 Buy plain papers as well as those with Christmas designs — they will help to create different effects and transform boxes into interesting shapes (see the little train and the shirt box on page 63).

3 Tissue paper makes good gift-wrap; wrap the box in a bright colour, fold and snip pieces from a second, paler colour and over-wrap the box for a lacy effect.

4 Children may not appreciate good gift papers — consider wrapping their gifts in pages from coloured comics, taped together, or bright wallpaper.

5 Newspaper. *The Times* in particular, makes an unusual — and smart — gift wrap, especially for a man. Tie the gift in bright red ribbon for contrast.

6 Pages from magazines or Sunday supplements can be used to make a collage gift-wrap. Choose advertisement or editorial pages with a large area of colour for the basic wrap. Cut and glue on from other pages, to make themes or motifs.

7 Personalise gifts with names and messages. Wrap the gift in a plain paper; cut letters from patterned paper, or use rub-on letters available from stationery shops.

8 Let children make their own gift paper; a pad of artist's layout paper will provide large-sized sheets. Half-potatoes or apples can be cut into designs for block-printing with poster colours, or try the effects of corks, pencil ends, pieces of sponge or cotton wool, string dipped in paint, bottle tops etc. Or, stencil patterns through paper doyleys with painting pens.

9 Cotton fabric makes a good 'wrap' for gifts and is especially useful for oddly-shaped presents. Use it over white tissue paper for the best effect.

11 Crafts foil is a little expensive but is ideal for small, awkwardly-shaped gifts, such as bottles, tins, or pencils. It is usually double-sided and left-over scraps can be used for a wide variety of decorative ornaments, such as holly leaves, bell-shapes, and stars.

12 Gold or silver doyleys, used over white or black tissue paper, can be used to wrap small, round gifts.

13 Sections cut from silver and gold doyleys add glitter to a package. Cut out the circular centres for 'snowflakes', cut motifs for gift tags, and use the lacy edges for a 'garland' round the edges of a box.

14 Write glittering messages with glue and glitter dust. Spread a line of glue thinly, sprinkle the dust and leave it to dry. A dry paint brush is useful for applying glitter dust in small quantities.

15 Use dressmaker's pinking shears for the edges of crêpe paper or tissue paper. Crêpe paper also pulls into a decorative edge — stretch it in between the fingers.

16 Use bits of last year's Christmas cards for making gift tags — but choose the areas carefully. Motifs can be cut out and glued to white, or coloured, card tags; cut out greetings and write personal messages on the other side. The secret is to measure and cut the tags very carefully for a professional look

Curling or crimping ribbon has a ribbed surface and is about 3 mm (1/8 inch) wide. Drawn over a knife blade it forms 'springs'. Gift ribbon that sticks to itself with a moistened finger tip makes easy bows and rosettes.

Cut 4 × 23 cm (9 inch) lengths and form them into figure-of-eights, sticking the ends together. Stick 'eights' together in twos, to make rosettes, then stick two rosettes together. Make a small loop for the middle.

(see the tags pictured on page 63). Punch holes in the tags and tie them on with narrow ribbon, or thread a large-eyed needle with gold crochet thread and 'sew' the tags on.

17 Use real woven satin ribbons to tie the gifts when you know the recipient will appreciate the ribbon as a 'second' gift.

18 Look for special 'cut-edge' gift ribbons, made from cotton and acetate fabrics: they come in festive prints and plain colours and tie beautiful bows. Some have glittering threads which pull the ribbons up into 'instant' bows.

19 For economical gift ties, consider glitter knitting wool, gold or silver crochet cotton, red parcel twine.

20 Special gifts need little wrapping, other than cellophane, if the container is part of the gift, for instance:
A flower pot containing a pair of gardening gloves, a packet or two of seeds for a gardener.
A china jelly mould with special packs of herbs or spices, and a pretty cook's apron, for a cook.
An inexpensive round basket, filled with small, perfumed soaps.
A growing plant, with small bows of gold ribbon tied to its branches.

21 Make your own gift bows and rosettes from ribbons or strips cut from gift wrap papers.

22 Awkwardly-shaped gifts need special treatment: Wrap

Gold, red and silver wrappings catch the festive atmosphere.
Attach contrasting boxes or ribbon roses (see page 58) for that special touch.

MULTI-BOW
Tie ribbon round the gift, making a double knot. Lay 3 or 4 × 10 cm (4 inch) pieces across the knot. Bring up the ribbon ends and knot over the pieces, pulling them into a multi-box.

23 Soft items, such as clothing, are best wrapped in a cracker shape. Roll the gift in tissue paper and tape it. Cut thin card to fit round the shape and half as long again. Tape it round the gift. Wrap in a large piece of gift paper, tie at the ends of the card to make a cracker shape. Fringe or pink the gift paper ends. Cut a decorative shape from another paper to decorate the cracker.

24 Cracker shapes are also good for long gifts of different kinds but pad the gift with tissue paper first.

25 Round gifts can either be tied in fabric or a soft paper, or tied into a 'second' gift, such as a scarf or a handkerchief. Alternatively, change the shape with corrugated card taped around the gift, then top-wrap.

26 Big items, such as a doll's house, can be wrapped in newspaper first, then decorated with brightly coloured, self-adhesive tape.

27 Put large gifts into a large plastic bag; black bin liners look good tied with red, white and green ribbons, or white swing-top bin liners can be decorated with shapes cut from coloured or foil papers. Wrap the gift in masses of brightly-coloured tissue paper first to mask its shape as much as possible.

28 Look at haberdashery counters for decorative trims — thick coloured cords, inexpensive nylon lace, Lurex braids, gold and silver buttons.

29 Stationers and art shops may have decorative items also — packs of fancy paper, shapes, or coloured spots, for making patterns on plain paper wrappings.

30 Tubes are useful 'boxes' for all kinds of gifts and simple to make. Roll the gift in thin cartridge paper or card and tape the join. Stand the tube on the card or paper and draw round the end. Cut out two circles, cutting out 12 mm (½ inch) from the drawn line. Using scissors, cut into the edge, up to the line. Spread a little glue on the cut 'tabs' and fit them carefully into the ends of the tube.

31 Collect boxes all through the year. To cover a box with gift paper, open up the box, separating the glued joins, and trace round the flat box, adding 12 mm (½ inch) all round. Spread glue on the extra 12 mm (½ inch) and fold it onto the flat box. Leave to dry, then glue the box back together again.

Kitchen foil makes a good gift-wrap for bottles.

bottles in tissue paper first, then a thin paper or filmwrap over the top, gathering the ends up round the neck. Snip the top edge into petal shapes, or fringe it; tie ornaments around the bottle neck; strings of glass beads, multi-bows of narrow ribbon etc.

STARBURST
Cut pieces of ribbon 10 cm (4 inch) long. Fishtail the ends or cut diagonally (round them off for a flower shape). Dampen the middle of each piece and twist it. Lay twists on top of each other, dampening them to secure. Use longer and smaller pieces for a different effect, and mix colours also. Ends can also be fringed.

CHRYSANTHEMUM
Lay ribbon in a zigzag pattern. Pick it up and twist wire round the middle. Pull out the petals.

32 Christmas stockings are fun for everyone. Make stockings from felt and use them from year to year, each member of the family having a special, personalised design, or make them disposable from inexpensive net. Machine-stitch the edges together over a strip of tissue paper, tearing it away afterwards, or stitch crêpe paper round the net stocking.

33 If gifts are to be posted, take time to pack them correctly. Stationers can provide stiff cardboard and corrugated card for strengthening boxes collected from supermarkets. Tape all the joins of the box first, then cut pieces of card to fit two opposite sides and the bottom in one piece, and then a second piece to cover the remaining opposite sides and bottom in one piece. Cut a piece of the stiffening card to fit on top of the gift.

34 Another way of using supermarket boxes is to cut off the flaps from two boxes of similar size. Put the gift in one box, place the second box over the top to make a lid. Tape the edges and tie with string before wrapping in strong brown paper.

35 It is better not to economise on packing material for posted gifts — the more you use, the more protection you provide for fragile or easily damaged items. Cellulose chips can sometimes be obtained from shops who sell TV sets or video recorders — alternatively, use quantities of torn-up newspaper or cotton wool.

An inviting pile of presents under the Christmas tree, for all the family

FLAT LOOP

Cut ribbon into 30, 25, 20 and 15 cm (12, 10, 8 and 6 inch) lengths. Dampen the ends and form the pieces into rings. Flatten the rings and dampen inside to form double loops. Stick loops one on another, the longest at the bottom, the smallest on top. Make a small loop on top to finish.

PRETTY PRESENTATIONS

· INDEX ·